TASTSTERONE™

THE BEST COOKBOOK FOR MEN

DEBRA LEVY PICARD

PHOTOGRAPHY BY STEPHAN LOWY

TASTOSTERONE: The Best Cookbook for Men

Tastosterone.com

This cookbook is dedicated to my
daughter Samantha, who is also
my toughest critic. If she requests
the same dinner again, I know it's a
winner; if she asks for leftovers for
breakfast, I also have a winner; if
she requests I make a meal for her
friends, it's a grand slam! I couldn't
have achieved this cookbook
without my daughter's support,
laughter, and discerning palate.

TASTOSTERONE™

THE BEST COOKBOOK FOR MEN

TABLE OF CONTENTS

WHY SHOULD MEN COOK?

TASTOSTERONE: The Best Cookbook for Men provides a man with a road map of simple recipes, tools, techniques, and tips for cooking. Just like men may choose to follow or ignore the directions on their navigation system, they are not expected to strictly follow the recipes in my cookbook. Experiment with flavors and taste test along the way. If you don't like olives, leave them out. If you like spicy foods, add a pinch of red pepper flakes. It's that easy!

The result of reading my cookbook could be three square meals a day or a quick breakfast on the weekend. Martha Stewart may have set the bar high for women across the country for years. Well, now I'm setting the bar low, expecting less, and getting great results from men in the kitchen.

So why do so many men avoid cooking? This important life skill not only instills a sexy confidence in a man, it also carries him through the highs and lows of life at any age. Whether for a lack of confidence, caring, or time, a man usually avoids cooking until absolutely necessary. TASTOSTERONE: The Best Cookbook for Men turns this need into a passion for cooking.

You may not know that PGA Golfer and Masters Tournament Winner Bubba Watson has never had a golf lesson. He taught himself to play as a kid by hitting wiffle balls in loops around his house. Bubba was fueled to play by a love of the sport. The same applies to cooking – once a man acquires a desire to cook, he'll be cooking through those courses.

We all know a man thrives off of a little competition! Once a man acquires some TASTOSTERONE, he can also try making a few of the Triple-T recipes at the end of some of my chapters to test his skills and impress the dinner guests. These recipes require the skill of a slightly more accomplished T-Man as well as some tools, technique and time (a Triple-T). After preparing a few simple T-Man recipes, men will find the confidence to flex those muscles and serve up TTT dishes with a new sexy swagger.

No matter how often you cook, you'll find that TASTOSTERONE: The Best Cookbook for Men is an essential part of every T-Man's culinary toolbox.

So now let's explore the various roles a man may find himself taking on throughout his life and why cooking would help him along the way.

THE YOUNG BOY

The time is now to create memories, promote healthy eating habits, and instill some TASTOSTERONE in your young boy. Many moms and dads prop their little girl on the counter and hand her a spoon so she can help mix the batter, scramble the eggs, and knead the dough. Why not do the same for your boys?

Boys deserve equal time in the kitchen and if you familiarize them with helping when they're young, they will develop a life-long passion for cooking. Your little chefs will also learn about math and teamwork by helping to set the table, serve food, clean the dishes, take measurements, and tell time. Rome wasn't built in a day, so start by having your son assist in the kitchen, then move on to simple no-fail recipes like my "You're in a Scramble" or grilled ham and cheese.

If you build a boy's confidence and pride, his culinary knowledge will grow with time. This boy will become a man soon enough so enjoy your priceless moments together getting messy, eating, and laughing in the kitchen. Who knows? Your little chef may just become the next Guy Fieri, Bobby Flay or Michael Symon.

THE TEENAGER

The adolescent's need to be independent drives a teenager, as well as frustrates parents. What better way to positively embrace a frustrated teen's insecurities than to build his confidence and independence through cooking? Due to hectic schedules, teens often find themselves heading out for fast food to satisfy their hunger. The athlete who runs five plus miles or plays two hours of football a day is famished long before dinner is served. Let's teach this teen to cook and prepare simple dishes that will satisfy his hunger.

Today's Mrs. Cleaver isn't at home waiting for her sons with a plate of warm cookies and milk. That scene is as much a thing of the past as Dad getting slippers and a pipe when he arrives home from work. Most parents work long hours and children should be taught to make themselves healthy, satisfying meals and snacks. Teenagers should be provided with the basic culinary skills needed to prepare a fast and filling meal or snack. While contending with growth spurts, academics, and recreational sports, a teenager requires fresh, healthy food to become a successful and happy individual. Simple snacks include recipes like my quick Great Guacamole and chips, or a sandwich from my chapter "Bag It", where he can learn to make a Panini sandwich with last night's leftover steak and some Parmesan cheese.

Remember to keep your kitchen stocked with a variety of foods so your teenager can assemble and prepare a meal or snack any time of the day. You never know, one day your TASTOSTERONE chef may even surprise you with dinner on the table.

THE COLLEGE STUDENT

Parents try to provide their sons with all the essentials when sending them off to college – money, books, bedding, and clothing. Why not a cookbook or two? A college freshman usually lives in dormitory housing where cafeteria food is less than desirable. However, there is no reason that this young man can't stock a small fridge in his room with a few culinary ingredients and have a school-approved hot plate. Arm your student with a little TASTOSTERONE and he will enjoy a satisfying collegiate career.

College is the beginning of a young man's adult life and knowing the basic skills of cooking will give him an advantage in school, at work and in home life. For example, your college student may find his knowledge of cooking makes it easier to secure a better paying job at a local restaurant or hotel. One added benefit of working in the food industry is the likely guarantee of free food. Let's not forget that cooking may also result in healthier eating habits, keeping off the freshman fifteen!

Providing young men with the skills, confidence and recipes to succeed in the kitchen are important lessons. Now, if I could just figure out how to help them make it through hazing and midterm exams! I am confident recipes like my "Bolognese" or "Swiss Mac and Cheese" will save the day.

THE SINGLE GUY

Spending most of his time working and socializing with friends, the single man eats on the go and is on a first name basis with the guy behind the deli counter or pizza joint. He pretty much avoids cooking all together, opting instead for a quick preservative-packed meal. This man is in desperate need of a home cooked meal. The single man may try to control every part of his life from the way his car is cleaned to the hours he puts in at the gym, so why does he leave cooking up to a stranger or the microwave?

TASTOSTERONE: The Best Cookbook for Men can come in handy for this man by building his confidence, saving him money, energizing him with healthy food, impressing the ladies, and ending his unhealthy friendship with the local delivery guy.

Inspired by the single guy's lack of time and patience, I wrote "Take Stock: Foods and Spices You Need," a chapter that makes a trip to the supermarket less intimidating and time-consuming. The single man should also note that women love a man who cooks and all is forgiven when he makes any one of the recipes in my chapter, "Dinner Darling." There is nothing sexier than a TASTOSTERONE man in the kitchen and a recipe like my "Swiss Fondue" takes no time at all to make, but he'll be enjoying the benefits from his simple culinary creation for weeks.

THE BOYFRIEND

Every woman has worn her boyfriend's shirt or jacket at one time or another. Borrowing and sporting his clothing are tangible reminders of your love for one another. Just like that piece of clothing, I hope women also enjoy borrowing my cookbook because I have found that there are some girlfriends out there in need of a little TASTOSTERONE. So feel free to sneak a peek, borrow and try a few of his recipes on for size. Whether you surprise him with "Grandma Barbara's Burgers" or "The Good Stuff," I guarantee you'll be as comfortable cooking these recipes as you are wearing his cozy flannel shirt.

Women, like men, sometimes need a little assistance in the kitchen. Ten or more years ago it was rare for a woman not to cook. Today's research shows women age 30 and under are taking on other roles and cooking is placed on the back burner to work and play.

THE NEWLYWED

After the happy couple has been toasted and the honeymoon is over, naturally they will begin dividing up the household chores. It may go something like this: he takes out the garbage and makes the morning coffee; she prepares his favorite foods and folds the laundry. Before setting up patterns that will most likely define roles in life, consider sharing the cooking. Define cooking as a skill, not a chore, by making time in the kitchen an important part of your shared daily routine initiated at the start of your marriage.

Come to think of it, wedding vows and prenuptials should include a mutual commitment to cook! Sharing the role of cook may prove more beneficial than you think. In addition to diving into a delicious meal each night, you will both enjoy conversation and a few laughs along the way. Both are important ingredients to a happy and healthy marriage. Start while you're newlyweds and there will be many stories and memories of culinary successes and failures for years to come.

To get started in the kitchen, plan a few easy meals you both crave or which remind you of your honeymoon, a dish eaten on your first date, or even the mouthwatering appetizer you enjoyed out on the town the night before. TASTOSTERONE will give you both the skills and confidence to master the art of cooking.

THE MARRIED MAN

How do you inspire a man who's been married for years and happily enjoys being on the receiving end of every meal to step foot in the kitchen? I may have my work cut out for me with the married man, but I'm confident that although set in his ways, all he requires is some motivation and a few incentives to get cooking in the kitchen.

During dinner with friends one night we were discussing the topic. One of the guys asked, "What would be in it for the husband if he cooked dinner?" I responded, "You're hungry, right? Well, you get a great dinner and, of course, you get brownie points that most wives happily redeem." My friend asked, "Do these points have blackout dates like airline rewards?" I laughed and responded,

"Maybe, but I guarantee the points earned from cooking adds miles to any marriage." That night we all ended the evening with a toast to racking up the frequent flyer brownie points and to long, happy marriages.

THE MANNY

Most of us are familiar with the role of a nanny thanks to the increased mainstream needs of today's full-time working parents. Mary Poppins, the most popular nanny of them all, not only disciplined children, but also taught them life lessons along the way. In recent years, the "manny" has become increasingly popular thanks to a rise in young men seeking alternate career choices. This new profession is teaching the important life lesson that the role of caregiver can be designated to either a male or female, changing the face of childcare forever.

The manny does just about everything from cleaning and schoolwork to playing sports. So why is he neglecting the cooking? If this manny can read and has the desire to eat then he can cook. A colleague of mine hired a manny years ago before it was Hollywood chic. This manny was great with his young boys; he had lots of energy and was always playing sports and horsing around with them till they were utterly exhausted. The manny is an asset to any family, especially one with active boys. However, we are all spoiled and everyone wants the entire package. He was amazing with the kids, but he didn't cook a lick and soon this active family became ravenous and tired of take-out. The manny must flex some TASTOSTERONE cooking muscles or his family will soon hunger for more.

MR. MOM

Your wife is the breadwinner of the family, traveling often and commuting long hours. You are the domestic dad. You volunteer at your kids' school, watch or coach games, help with homework, and wash and fold the laundry. Don't forget, with such a busy, working wife, you will also have to cook the meals. What! Cook? Okay, Mister Mom, you can do this: pizza delivery on Monday, Chinese take-out on Tuesday, fast food burgers on Wednesday, frozen something on Thursday, etc. and repeat. Stop here!

Soon, you'll find out that fast food doesn't work and these quick food fixes result in a house full of cranky, tired children who trudge around begging for home cooked, delicious meals. Okay, so they might not plead with you to bust out the healthy meals or snacks because most kids love the junk, but you owe it to your kids to set an example of healthy eating habits. You've taught them how to throw a ball and study for a test, and now it's time to teach them how to make and enjoy a nutritious meal. TASTOSTERONE and healthy eating habits can be passed down, so let's work on tomorrow today.

THE WIDOWER

One day I ran into a good friend and fellow foodie who was in town for a visit from London. He had lost his wife to cancer a few years earlier. She was an exceptional wife and mother who conquered life with effortless grace and determination. Whether organizing a dinner party for friends, skiing the Swiss Alps, or hiking Mount Kilimanjaro, she was naturally amazing at everything. Since her passing, her husband has assumed the roles of both mom and dad and has done a phenomenal job raising their teenage son.

On a recent trip to the supermarket, his son asked if they could avoid the microwave food aisle. "Sure," my friend said. "Let's go to prepared foods." I have a feeling this was not what his son meant at all! Knowing how much I love to cook, he admitted to me that while handling what life had dealt him he's put cooking on the back burner so to speak. He knows he can't, and doesn't want to attempt the mouthwatering recipes his wife used to prepare. But he also knows that cooking is another skill that he must acquire so that his son will learn to enjoy an independent, healthy lifestyle. Since my friend has already conquered the running of the bulls and Mount Kilimanjaro with his adventurous wife, gaining some TASTOSTERONE should be a cinch, not an uphill battle.

A great place to start, especially if you have a teenager, is by working together. A panini maker is a fun, fast and foolproof tool to satisfy a hungry teenager's appetite. Or, a new cook can always start out slowly by just scrambling up some eggs and toasting some bread to get comfortable in the kitchen. Then he can move on to some of my B.Y.O.B. recipes in Chapter 4 and impress himself and his new dinner guests. Just like the baby steps this family needed to take to heal emotionally, they will also need to take the same small steps to enjoy making new memories together, cooking as a family.

THE DIVORCÉ

Remember the movie "Mrs. Doubtfire" in which actor Robin Williams disguised himself as a nanny to gain more time with his children? After "Mrs. Doubtfire" attempted to prepare a dinner and burned it, he ordered an expensive meal from a restaurant and pretended to make it himself to impress his ex-wife and children. However, by the end of the film, he was able to prepare simple delicious meals and also had a sense of pride and confidence in himself that made him a "different" man.

When a man goes through a divorce he may need to develop skills that he has never used or may be a bit rusty on, and no, I'm not referring to dating. It takes a special TASTOSTERONE guy to cook for himself and his children. It's easy for a divorced man to treat himself to fancy dinners, expensive takeout, and prepared foods. Men find these foods appealing because they are loaded with salt, fat, and preservatives. But does the divorced man really care about what he's placing in his mouth? Well, if you do, start taking control of your life by controlling what you eat. The enjoyment of great food is a definite side effect of gaining some TASTOSTERONE, but so is a certain confident swagger.

THE RETIRED MAN

So you've worked for the past hundred years (at least if feels that way) and now you're ready to retire. There's no clock to punch, no boss to answer to (except maybe your wife) and employees are a thing of the past. You may decide to spend your golden years enjoying the warm sun and sand of Florida, traveling to foreign places, or watching your grandchildren grow up. Whatever the plan, I'm certain food is going to be part of it.

My parents opted to move to Florida where they enjoy playing golf and bridge, attending concerts and socializing with friends. Yes, they are very busy and love

the retired years. My dad's transitional life from full-time boss of his own business to full-time retiree was quite an adjustment. Newly retired married couples assume new roles and it may take time and patience for them to blend as a couple again. Luckily, my parents found that balance and I believe they are deeper in love now than ever (if that's even possible).

So what does this retired couple's love story have to do with TASTOSTERONE? By spending much more time together, meals have become an important part of their daily routine with more planning and time socializing. My dad is finding that gone are the days of the working lunch and sandwiches on-the-go. Retired men are spending more time with their wives, engaging in conversation, and sharing household duties. With that said, I see a little (or a lot) of TASTOSTERONE in a retired man's future.

Several years ago, my parents' long-time friends Jerry and Eva invited our family to their home for dinner the evening before Thanksgiving. The night's preparations were a team effort with both of them setting the table and preparing delicious salmon, salads, fresh asparagus, roast chicken, and more. However, the pièce de résistance that evening was what Jerry called his "famous chicken chili." Other common adjectives men use to describe their culinary creations are "world famous" and "the one-and-only." Jerry proudly served his chili with that TASTOSTERONE swagger in his "special" bowls accompanied by freshly grated cheese and some chopped onion. He awaited the accolades as we all ate.

Their meal was delicious. This retired dynamic duo served up an outstanding healthy meal in the comfort of their very own kitchen. The best part was that there were no waiters to interrupt our great conversation or background noise to make it difficult to hear each other. For most people over 65 hearing loss comes with the territory and repeating a conversation about ten times over the course of a meal can get old.

Both Jerry and my father found TASTOSTERONE in their retirement years. Their love of food, family, and home inspired them to drum up the confidence and courage to cook. My dad also now enjoys shopping at the supermarket, something he had never done before on his own. He loves hunting for the next treasure, an ingredient that my mother would have never discovered in a million years. And, most importantly, thanks to his newfound culinary independence, he never waits on mom to prepare a meal. He makes his own breakfast and cooks up a mean lunch.

Since I began writing this book several years ago, I've had the pleasure of hearing dozens of heart-warming retirement stories from friends and family. The one that touched me the most was about a man in his 90's who had been baking his entire life. As a child, he used to help his mom in the kitchen and would rush through his homework so he would have time in the evening to bake with her and enjoy those special times together. "Baking," he said, "Keeps my mind sharp, reminds me of my childhood and now gives me great memories and recipes to pass down to my grandchild." I think it's important for a retired man to pick up a new hobby or rekindle a long lost one.

A man's role may change throughout his life, but no matter what life dishes out, cooking will always nurture and feed his soul. With a healthy dose of gentle reassurance and humor, TASTOSTERONE helps men to heal, celebrate and laugh by way of cooking.

I hope you enjoy reading and trying out the recipes in TASTOSTERONE: The Best Cookbook for Men. My book should meet your culinary needs at any stage of life. Keep in mind, if you ever have a question, feel free to tweet me @Tastosterone. There is no shame in stopping and asking for directions.

A man's role may change throughout his life, but no matter what life dishes out cooking will always nurture and feed his soul. With a healthy dose of gentle reassurance and humor, TASTOSTERONE helps men to heal, celebrate and laugh by way of cooking.

Debbie

CHICKEN BITES
Page 25

SHRIMP & CRAB DIP
Page 9

GREAT GUACAMOLE
Page 11

WORTH IT CHICKEN STOCK
Page 29

STUFFED CLAMS
Page 15

CHAPTER 1

JUST START: SOUPS & STARTERS

Starters usually have a feminine appeal, but don't let these dainty finger foods fool you for a second. They can entertain a large crowd of football fans or a ravenous pack of teenagers for hours.

Once the TASTOSTERONE man gets into the swing of cooking my starters, he may just ditch the main course altogether and enjoy satisfying simple meals packed with plenty of flavor.

WHATEVER VEGETABLE SOUP

Soup's on! I can eat soup every day for lunch or dinner. This soup is especially great because it's a seasonal dish that you can make with many different kinds of vegetables. Adding the meat from rotisserie chicken leftovers can also add lots of flavor. The house is guaranteed to smell amazing when you make this soup!

Servings: **6**

Prep Time: **30 minutes**

Cook Time: **40 minutes**

INGREDIENTS

2 tablespoons olive oil

1 onion, chopped

1 leek, white parts only, chopped

3 carrots, diced

4 stalks of celery, diced

Shredded cooked chicken (optional)

1 pound mushrooms, sliced

8 cups low sodium chicken stock, store bought or from scratch (see page 29 for my chicken stock recipe)

1/2 cup white wine

One 15-ounce can diced tomatoes (I prefer fire roasted)

1-2 tablespoons tomato paste

2 tablespoons heavy cream

Salt and pepper

THE WHATEVER

These ingredients depend on what you feel like throwing in or have on hand.

Beans (I use white or garbanzo beans)

Zucchini or yellow squash, half-moon sliced

Green beans

Shredded cabbage

Peas

Pearl onions

Roasted vegetables (these may also available in the prepared foods section)

Fresh herbs (I use basil, parsley, dill, and thyme)

Parmesan cheese, grated

Red pepper flakes

SHOPPING LIST

Need
- [ ] Chicken stock
- [ ] Carrots
- [ ] Celery
- [ ] Onion
- [ ] Leek
- [ ] Mushrooms
- [ ] Diced tomatoes
- [ ] Tomato Paste
- [ ] Heavy cream

May Have on Hand
- [ ] Olive oil
- [ ] White wine
- [ ] Salt and pepper

Optional
- [ ] Shredded chicken

DIRECTIONS

1. Heat oil in a large soup pot.
2. Add onions, leeks, carrots, and celery. Cook for 10 minutes on medium heat. Add mushrooms and any other vegetables. Cook for an additional 5 minutes. Reduce to a low heat.
3. Add white wine, tomato paste and chopped tomatoes. Cook for 3 minutes.
4. Add chicken stock and shredded chicken (optional). Bring to a boil.
5. Cover and reduce heat to a simmer for 20 minutes.
6. Add cream, salt and pepper to taste.
7. Serve warm with grated Parmesan cheese and red pepper flakes on the side.

TIP

Leeks can be very dirty. Make deep long cuts, run them thoroughly under water, and shake them out before you slice them.

STEAKHOUSE ONION SOUP

There is something about a bowl of onion soup that warms the soul. I've been making this dish forever and still serve it in the bowls my mom gave me years ago. Keep in mind, adding cheese to your soup also adds salt and this may be the reason why I'm not a fan of onion soup when I order it out. You'll find that when you make your own onion soup you have more control over its flavor.

INGREDIENTS

3 tablespoons unsalted butter

6 large yellow onions, sliced

1/4 cup sugar

1 teaspoon black pepper

4 cups low sodium beef stock

4 cups regular beef stock

1 bay leaf

1/4 cup port wine

6 slices of French bread

3 cups Gruyère cheese, shredded

DIRECTIONS

1. Melt butter in a large soup pot or a large sauté pan.
2. Add sliced onions and cook covered over low flame for 20 minutes. Add sugar and continue to cook uncovered for an additional 20 minutes or until the onions caramelize. (Do not crowd onions or they will soften and not caramelize.)
3. Add port wine, broth, bay leaf and pepper.
4. Simmer for 30 - 40 minutes covered.
5. Remove bay leaf.
6. Preheat oven to broil.
7. Place ovenproof soup bowls on baking sheet lined with foil.
8. Distribute broth and onion in each bowl. Place bread in at an angle and top with cheese.
9. Broil for 5 minutes or until cheese melts. You can also bake soup for 10 minutes in a 350°F oven.

Servings: **6**

Prep Time: **20 minutes**

Cook Time: **1 hour**

SHOPPING LIST

Need
- ☐ Beef stock (low sodium)
- ☐ Beef stock (regular)
- ☐ Gruyère cheese
- ☐ Yellow onions
- ☐ French bread
- ☐ Port wine

May Have on Hand
- ☐ Butter
- ☐ Bay leaf
- ☐ Pepper
- ☐ Sugar

TIPS

Slow and low! Be certain flame is low when cooking the soup, or your onions will never caramelize.

The soup bowls will be very hot. Handle them with oven mitts only. No, really... don't be a hero and grab them with your bare hands!

PROSCIUTTO AND MELON

My mother introduced me to the taste sensation of prosciutto and melon when I was ten years old. My parents traveled often and their cooking incorporated many of the dishes enjoyed on their trips. Today, Prosciutto di Parma, is readily available at your local grocery store or Italian delicatessen. I serve this dish with fresh Italian bread and a glass of vino. Mangia!

Servings: **4**

Prep Time: **5 minutes**

Cook Time: **None**

INGREDIENTS

1 cantaloupe or honeydew, cubed or sliced

10 slices Prosciutto di Parma, thinly sliced

1 fresh lemon

Salt and freshly ground black pepper

DIRECTIONS

1. Place the sliced or cubed fresh melon on a plate.

2. Layer the Prosciutto di Parma over the melon.

3. Add fresh ground pepper to taste and top with a squeeze of fresh lemon.

4. Serve immediately.

TIPS

Color and aroma are the best guides to selecting cantaloupe. They should have a delicate aroma and thick netting over a yellow skin. Smell it! If it smells like a melon, it's good to eat.

SHOPPING LIST

Need

☐ Cantaloupe or honeydew

☐ Prosciutto di Parma

May Have on Hand

☐ Lemon

☐ Salt and pepper

SHRIMP & CRAB DIP

Eating some fresh shrimp and crabmeat is a great way to get that lean extra protein boost. If you're in a pinch you can always use the canned stuff. Don't forget to drain the liquid first or your seafood will be swimming around in watery dip!

INGREDIENTS

12 ounces fresh cleaned and cooked shrimp, roughly chopped

12 ounces fresh crabmeat (pick through to take out any shells)

1/2 cup mayonnaise (I prefer Hellman's brand)

6 ounces cream cheese, softened

2 tablespoons hot or sweet and tangy sauce (my new favorites are Fourth Creek Sweet Red Pepper Relish and Mazi Piri Piri Sauce)

DIRECTIONS

1. Mix all the ingredients together.

2. Add salt and pepper to taste.

3. Refrigerate then serve with chips, crackers or fresh raw vegetables.

Servings: **8 - 10**

Prep Time: **5 minutes**

Cook Time: **None**

SHOPPING LIST

Need

☐ Crabmeat

☐ Cream cheese

☐ Shrimp

May Have on Hand

☐ Hot or sweet and tangy sauce

☐ Mayonnaise

GREAT GUACAMOLE

Fruit or vegetable? The avocado is a gift from the heavens. Eat this fruit plain or with salt and pepper. You can also doctor it up with chopped red onion, garlic, tomato, and some lemon or lime juice.

INGREDIENTS

4 ripe avocados (I prefer Haas avocados)

Sea salt (or any salt on hand) and freshly ground black pepper

Juice from one lemon or lime

3 springs fresh cilantro, chopped or 1 tablespoon dried cilantro (optional)

DIRECTIONS

1 On a cutting board, slice avocado in half and remove the pit. Knife out the avocado pit. (See page 253.) Discard pit and skin.

2 Put avocado in bowl and mash with a fork.

3 Season with salt, pepper, and lemon or lime juice. Mix in cilantro.

4 Add any other ingredients of choice. (I prefer chopped tomato, red onion, and garlic.)

5 Serve with chips or as a side, complimenting grilled chicken, fish or steak. Use your imagination – guacamole goes well with many dishes.

TIPS

Avocados vary in size, shape and color from green to black. Brown markings on skin do not lower quality. Rip off stem on top of fruit and if it's brown, it's also brown inside and no good.

Avocado oxidizes quickly so keep the pit in the mixture to stop the browning or use lemon or lime juice to slow down the process.

This dish is best made right before serving, but leave at least 5 minutes for the seasonings to blend.

Servings: **4**

Prep Time: **10 minutes**

Cook Time: **10 minutes**

SHOPPING LIST

Need

☐ Avocados

☐ Cilantro

May Have on Hand

☐ Lemon or lime

☐ Salt and pepper

Optional

☐ Tomato

☐ Red Onion

☐ Garlic

BAKED BEANS AND FRANKS

This dish is doggone easy to cook. Don't be a wiener and change this one much. Why mess with a classic?

Servings: **8**

Prep Time: **5 minutes**

Cook Time: **1 hour**

INGREDIENTS

1-pound mini hot dogs

2 small 8-ounce cans of tomato sauce

2 tablespoons brown sugar

1 tablespoon dry mustard

1 teaspoon Worcestershire sauce

Two 15-ounce cans of baked beans (if beans are in sauce omit one can of tomato sauce)

DIRECTIONS

1. Preheat oven to 350°F.
2. In a large oven proof casserole dish, mix all ingredients together then stir in the mini hotdogs.
3. Cover and bake for 1 hour.
4. Serve as an appetizer or on buns for some Sloppy Dogs, a twist on the traditional Sloppy Joe.

TIP

Freeze your leftover buns. When ready to use, wrap them in foil and pop them in the toaster oven set to 350°. Let them heat up for a minimum of ten minutes. The insides of the bread will continue to defrost.

SHOPPING LIST

Need

☐ Mini hot dogs

☐ Tomato sauce

☐ Baked beans

May Have on Hand

☐ Brown sugar

☐ Dry mustard

☐ Worcestershire sauce

BAKED STUFFED CLAMS

This recipe is perfect for an afternoon football game or a casual dinner. Serve stuffing in individual clamshells or as a warm dip with fresh French bread or crackers.

INGREDIENTS

Two 6-ounce cans of clams, minced or chopped
   (reserve 1/4 cup of the clam juice)
4 garlic cloves, minced
4 tablespoons olive oil
1 small yellow onion, peeled and chopped
2 tablespoons fresh parsley, chopped
1 teaspoon dry oregano
1/2 cup seasoned breadcrumbs
1/3 cup Parmesan cheese, grated
Juice of two lemons
Two dozen clamshells, roughly 2-3 inches in diameter
Salt and pepper

DIRECTIONS

1 Preheat oven to 300°F.
2 Preheat medium sauté pan over medium heat.
3 Add olive oil, garlic, onion, parsley, oregano, and drained clams. Sauté for 3 minutes.
4 Mix in breadcrumbs, cheese, reserved clam juice, juice of one lemon, and salt and pepper to taste. Mixture should hold together. Add a little more cheese or breadcrumbs if needed.
5 Spoon into clamshells or a 6-inch round oven safe casserole dish.
6 Place clamshells or dish on baking sheet.
7 Top each clam with a pinch of Parmesan cheese and a squeeze of fresh lemon juice.
8 Bake for 20 minutes.
9 Serve warm with slices of fresh lemon and garnish with chopped parsley.

Servings: **4**

Prep Time: **15 minutes**

Cook Time: **20 minutes**

SHOPPING LIST

Need
☐ Clams
☐ Clamshells
☐ Garlic
☐ Lemons
☐ Onion
☐ Parsley
☐ Parmesan cheese

May Have on Hand
☐ Breadcrumbs
☐ Olive oil
☐ Oregano
☐ Salt and pepper

TIPS

Ask your fishmonger for empty clamshells. When you bring them home, soak them in water and white wine vinegar, then scrub them clean and dry.

After draining the clam juice, a little dirt may settle at the bottom of the bowl. Make sure you don't pour the dirt into the clam mixture.

SHRIMP CHORIZO PAELLA KABOBS

Servings: 4

Prep Time: **20 minutes**

Cook Time: **5 minutes**

Paella is one of my favorite meals. There are so many versions of this traditional Spanish dish and very little that can go wrong when cooking it. Traditional paella recipes require large crowds, but when made into kabobs you can enjoy this flavorful recipe with just a few friends.

INGREDIENTS

6 links uncooked Mexican chorizo (peel off casing and cut into 1-inch slices)

20 uncooked large shrimp, cleaned and deveined

2 green peppers, cut into large cubes

2 tablespoons olive oil

Juice of 1 lemon

1 tablespoon fresh cilantro, chopped or 1 teaspoon dried cilantro

Salt and pepper

Wooden skewers

SHOPPING LIST

Need

☐ Chorizo

☐ Cilantro

☐ Green peppers

☐ Shrimp

☐ Wooden skewers

May Have on Hand

☐ Lemon

☐ Olive oil

☐ Salt and pepper

DIRECTIONS

1. Mix all the ingredients together in a bowl.
2. Refrigerate for 20 minutes. (No longer or shrimp will become mealy.)
3. While mixture is in the refrigerator, soak wooden skewers on a long flat plate with enough water to cover them. Soaking will ensure that the skewers do not burn when cooked. If skewers tend to float, just place another plate over them to weigh them down.
4. Alternate threading shrimp, chorizo, and pepper on the skewers. Sauté in a hot pan or on a grill plate for 2 minutes each side.
5. Add salt and pepper to taste. (Remember to season when hot so the seasoning will stick.)
6. Serve with rice as a main course or on the skewer as a light dinner or starter.

TIPS

You can purchase cleaned and deveined shrimp. I prefer to cook shrimp with tails on.

Mexican chorizo (pork sausage) is usually made with chili peppers and has a smoother appearance than Spanish chorizo.

SCALLOPS WRAPPED IN BACON

This is a classic appetizer. Remember, everything tastes better with bacon.

INGREDIENTS

1 pound sea scallops (I prefer the larger sea scallops to the smaller bay scallops)

1 pound bacon strips

1/2 tablespoon olive oil

DIRECTIONS

1 Preheat oven to 350°F.

2 Line a baking sheet with non-stick foil.

3 Cut bacon strips in half with kitchen scissors. Wrap a slice of cut bacon around each scallop and fasten with a toothpick by sticking it through the bacon and the scallop.

4 Place on a baking sheet.

5 Drizzle with olive oil.

6 Bake for 20 minutes or until bacon is crisp and golden.

7 Place on paper towels to drain excess oil.

8 Plate, serve and enjoy.

Servings: **6**

Prep Time: **10 minutes**

Cook Time: **20 minutes**

SHOPPING LIST

Need

☐ Bacon

☐ Scallops

May Have on Hand

☐ Olive oil

☐ Toothpicks

LAMB CHOP BITES

If you're downsizing for the holidays or serving this dish as an appetizer for a large party, your technique and skills will impress the guests. I also serve this dish as a simple meal with a side salad.

INGREDIENTS

15 one to two ounce mini lamb chops

1 teaspoon pepper

1/2 teaspoon salt

1 tablespoon garlic, chopped

1 tablespoon fresh oregano, chopped or 4 teaspoons dried oregano

1/4 cup olive oil

Cheese, shredded or grated (optional) (I prefer Parmesan, goat, blue or Gorgonzola)

Soy sauce (optional)

DIRECTIONS

1 Mix all ingredients together except the lamb chops, and place in a large bowl.

2 Add chops to mixture and marinate for 30 minutes.

3 Preheat sauté pan until very hot.

4 Add chops and marinade to hot pan. Sear 3 minutes on each side until desired doneness.

5 Remove from pan and place on a serving plate.

6 Sprinkle with salt and pepper to taste.

7 Cover plate with foil and rest meat for 5 minutes.

8 Sprinkle with cheese or a dash of soy sauce while chops are hot (optional).

Servings: **4**

Prep Time: **35 minutes**

Cook Time: **6 minutes**

SHOPPING LIST

Need

☐ Garlic

☐ Mini lamb chops

☐ Oregano

May Have on Hand

☐ Olive oil

☐ Salt and pepper

Optional

☐ Cheese

☐ Soy sauce

TIP

If you prefer a less gamey taste, presoak your lamb chops in milk for a maximum of two hours and refrigerate until you are ready to cook.

KEFTKA LAMB MEATBALLS

The Keftka is a Middle Eastern lamb meatball. This dish is a variation of a traditional Moroccan-style recipe. It's a flavorful dish sure to spice up any evening at home.

Servings: **4-6**

Prep Time: **15 minutes**

Cook Time: **20 minutes**

INGREDIENTS

2 tablespoons olive oil
1 small onion, chopped
2 tablespoons flat leaf parsley, chopped
2 tablespoons cilantro, chopped
1 teaspoon cumin
1 teaspoon sweet paprika
1/2 teaspoon cayenne pepper
1 teaspoon salt
1 pound ground lamb
1 package wooden skewers

DIRECTIONS

1. Preheat broiler.
2. In small non-stick pan over low heat, sauté the onion in olive oil until soft, for about 10 minutes.
3. In a large bowl, add onions and mix together all ingredients.
4. Form meat into balls similar in shape to mini-footballs.
5. Place meatballs on broiling pan lined with aluminum foil and cook for 10 minutes.
6. Remove from broiler, dab with paper towels to remove excess oil and place on skewers.
7. Serve with yogurt/cucumber dressing and/or chopped salad.

GREEK STYLE YOGURT DRESSING

2 cups Greek style plain yogurt
1 seedless cucumber, chopped
2 tablespoons fresh dill, chopped

1. Mix together all ingredients.
2. Serve on the side with grilled meat or fish.

SHOPPING LIST

Need
- ☐ Ground lamb
- ☐ Onion
- ☐ Cucumber
- ☐ Cilantro
- ☐ Dill
- ☐ Parsley (flat leaf)
- ☐ Greek yogurt
- ☐ Wooden skewers

May Have on Hand
- ☐ Olive oil
- ☐ Cayenne pepper
- ☐ Cumin
- ☐ Sweet paprika
- ☐ Salt

CHICKEN BITES

This will be your T-Man go-to dish no matter if you're cooking for your wife, the kids or fellow bachelors. Chicken bites are always a win-win.

INGREDIENTS

1 pound skinless and boneless chicken breasts cut into large strips
  (your butcher can do this for you)
1/2 cup flour
1/2 cup seasoned breadcrumbs
1 egg
1 tablespoon water
1/2 cup Parmesan cheese, grated
2 tablespoons butter
2 tablespoons olive oil
2 tablespoons sesame seeds
1 bottle plum sauce
Salt and pepper

DIRECTIONS

1 Preheat oven to 350°F.

2 Place flour in a bowl and season with salt and pepper.

3 In another bowl, create an egg wash by adding one lightly beaten egg to water. Season with salt and pepper.

4 Place breadcrumbs and Parmesan cheese in a third bowl. Toss to combine.

5 Dip chicken into flour, then egg, then breadcrumbs and Parmesan cheese. Set aside on a plate.

6 Heat a large non-stick sauté pan with oil and butter over medium heat.

7 Add breaded chicken strips to oil and butter. Cook for 3 minutes per side or until golden brown. Add additional butter and olive oil if liquid reduces.

8 Remove from pan.

9 Season with salt, pepper and sesame seeds.

10 Place on foil-lined baking sheet and bake for 15 minutes.

11 Serve with plum sauce.

Servings: **4**

Prep Time: **15 minutes**

Cook Time: **20 minutes**

SHOPPING LIST

Need
☐ Chicken breasts
☐ Plum sauce
☐ Parmesan cheese
☐ Sesame seeds

May Have on Hand
☐ Flour
☐ Egg
☐ Breadcrumbs
☐ Butter
☐ Olive oil
☐ Salt and pepper

TIP

A great way to remember this recipe's directions is to think of the TASTOSTERONE term FEB: one bowl with flour, one bowl with egg wash, and one bowl with breadcrumbs. (See page 257.)

WING IT

Wings are a favorite appetizer at restaurants and sports bars. Here's my own recipe for a dish that recreates this fan favorite. So wing it and enjoy!

INGREDIENTS

Three 1-pound packages of chicken wings (I prefer smaller wings like Perdue's Wingettes)
5 tablespoons butter
1/2 cup hot sauce (I prefer Cholula hot sauce)
3/4 cup flour
1/2 teaspoon cayenne pepper
1 teaspoon chili pepper
1/2 teaspoon garlic powder
1/4 teaspoon hot paprika
1/2 teaspoon salt
1/4 teaspoon black pepper
Blue cheese dressing (I opt for refrigerated blue cheese dressing)
Celery sticks

DIRECTIONS

1 In a very large saucepan melt the butter. Add hot sauce, turn off heat, and leave on stove for use later when you will add the wings.

2 In a large plastic bag mix the flour and remaining ingredients.

3 Add a few wings at a time to the bag of flour and shake. Remove wings from the flour, shake off excess flour, and set aside in large bowl. Repeat until all the wings are coated.

4 Cover bowl with plastic wrap then place wings in refrigerator for 30 minutes.

5 Line a baking sheet with aluminum foil.

6 Preheat oven to 425°F.

7 Place chilled wings in room temperature butter and hot sauce mixture that was set aside on the stove. Do not heat. Toss wings until coated.

8 Transfer wings to baking sheet.

9 Bake in oven for 20 minutes per side until golden brown.

10 Remove from oven and place in a large bowl.

11 Serve with blue cheese dressing and celery sticks.

Servings: **6-8**

Prep Time: **20 minutes**

Cook Time: **40 minutes**

SHOPPING LIST

Need
☐ Chicken wings
☐ Blue cheese dressing
☐ Celery

May Have on Hand
☐ Butter
☐ Hot sauce
☐ Flour
☐ Cayenne pepper
☐ Garlic powder
☐ Hot paprika
☐ Chili pepper
☐ Salt and pepper

TIP

To change the flavor of your wings, switch out your hot sauce with soy sauce, teriyaki, plum sauce, or apricot jam.

WORTH IT CHICKEN STOCK

Why make chicken stock when it's a snap to pick up at the store? Well, the answer is simple: it just tastes better. Soup can be the star of any meal when you go the extra mile and make homemade stock. Once I was carrying a full pot of stock to my downstairs freezer and I tripped. Stock flew everywhere! Needless to say, I wasn't happy, but the next day I went back to the drawing board and made a new batch. After all, it is called "Worth it Chicken Stock." It's that good!

INGREDIENTS

Two 3-pound chickens (ask butcher to cut up chicken in four pieces with skin on and discard gizzards and livers)
3 chicken breasts, bone-in with skin
2 large yellow onions with skin on
5 carrots, unpeeled and snapped in half
5 celery stalks, snapped in half
2 turnips, cut in half
1 leek, dirt removed, sliced, and quartered
1 head garlic, sliced in half with skin on
6 sprigs/bunch fresh Italian parsley
6 sprigs/bunch fresh thyme
6 sprigs/bunch fresh dill
1 tablespoon sea salt
3 teaspoons peppercorns

Additional ingredients if making chicken soup:
5 carrots, peeled and chopped
5 celery stalks, chopped
2- 3 sprigs fresh dill, chopped (optional)
1 pound cooked egg noodles (follow cooking directions on box)

DIRECTIONS

1 Place all ingredients in a very large stockpot (about 20 quarts). Fill with water to cover.
2 Bring to a boil.
3 Let simmer uncovered for 3 hours, adding water if broth gets low.
4 If making chicken soup, remove chicken breasts after 30 - 40 minutes and set aside to cool. If you're not making chicken soup just leave the breasts in the pot to add additional flavor to the stock.
5 After 3 hours strain liquid and discard remains. Empty clear liquid into a clean pot.
6 Let cool then place stock in a container. Store in refrigerator or freezer. If making chicken soup, add chicken from Step 4, carrots, celery, and dill (optional) to stock. Heat for 10 minutes, then serve with cooked noodles.

Servings: **12**

Prep Time: **10 minutes**

Cook Time: **3 hours**

SHOPPING LIST

Need

☐ Chickens (whole)
☐ Chicken breasts
☐ Carrots
☐ Celery
☐ Onions
☐ Leek
☐ Garlic
☐ Turnips
☐ Italian parsley (fresh)
☐ Thyme (fresh)
☐ Dill (fresh)

May Have on Hand

☐ Sea salt
☐ Peppercorns

Optional

☐ Egg noodles

TIP

Take stock! Cook noodles separately and do not add them to the soup until ready to serve because they will absorb the stock.

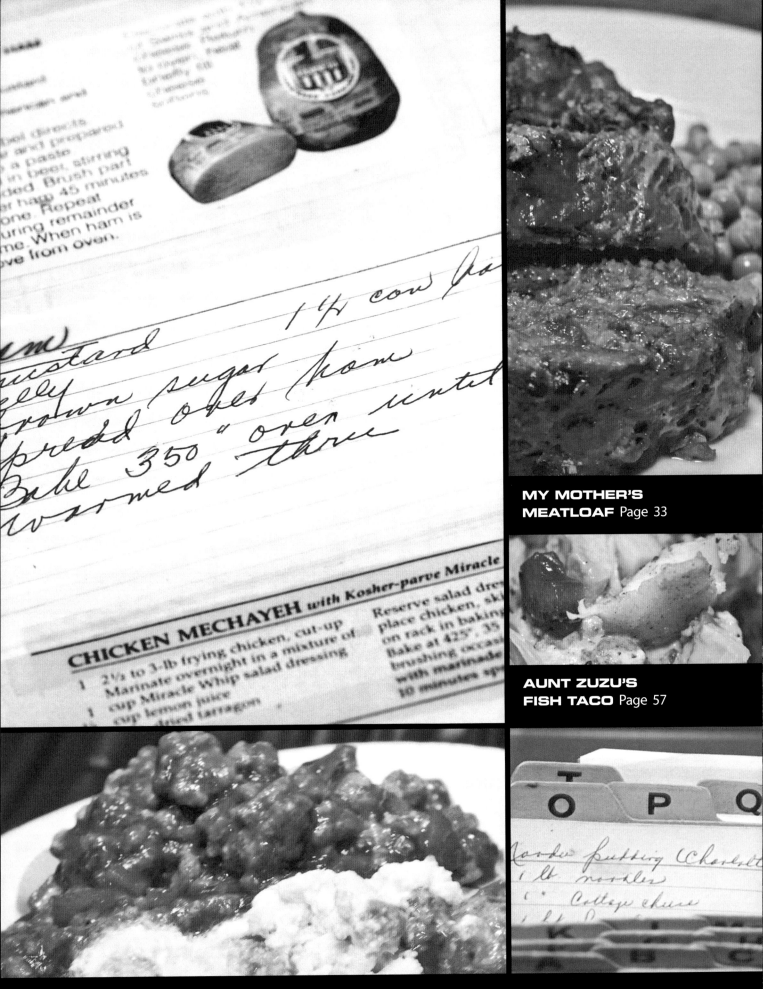

CHICKEN MECHAYEH with Kosher-parve Miracle

1 2½ to 3-lb frying chicken, cut-up
Marinate overnight in a mixture of
1 cup Miracle Whip salad dressing
cup lemon juice
dried tarragon

Reserve salad dres
place chicken, ski
on rack in baking
Bake at 425°, 35
brushing occas
with marinade
10 minutes sp

**MY MOTHER'S
MEATLOAF** Page 33

**AUNT ZUZU'S
FISH TACO** Page 57

DEBRA'S BEST BOLOGNESE
Page 59

CHAPTER 2

HOMAGE TO MOM: PASS IT DOWN

Men owe their nostalgia for certain foods to memories of mom cooking in the kitchen. In this chapter, I pay homage to my family's recipes by passing them down to the TASTOSTERONE cook so he too can enjoy them for years to come. "Homage to Mom" will give a man the confidence and skills needed to create the meals that serve as the meat and potatoes of his cooking repertoire. All the recipes are mom approved.

A first-time cook can start with any one of these dinners and impress even the most difficult family judge, mother-in-law included. They will be warming up to your home-cooked meals in no time, asking for the recipes for your family favorites. Start with "My Mother's Meatloaf" or "Classic Parmesan Chicken" and begin the tradition of cooking in your own home.

This chapter may also inspire the TASTOSTERONE man to spend a day with his own mom, learning her dishes so he too can pass them down. Not every family has a daughter, making it necessary for the TASTOSTERONE chef to honor mom by sharing her knowledge and recreating those nostalgic smells of comfort foods he fondly remembers from childhood.

MY MOTHER'S MEATLOAF

Everyone remembers meatloaf night. It's the ultimate in comfort food and also makes the best sandwiches the next day. My mom serves her meatloaf with a tomato sauce, mashed potatoes and frozen baby peas. It's the absolute best version around!

Compliments of mom, home cooking doesn't get better than this dish!

INGREDIENTS

3 slices of bread
1/2 cup milk
1/2 cup seasoned breadcrumbs
1/2 cup Parmesan cheese, shredded or grated
2 pounds meatloaf mix (a combination of ground veal, pork, and beef)
1 onion, chopped
3 tablespoons parsley, chopped
2 garlic cloves, minced
1 egg slightly beaten
3/4 cup ketchup plus 1/4 cup as topping
Salt and pepper

DIRECTIONS

1. Preheat oven to 400°F.
2. Sauté onion, garlic and parsley for 4 minutes in pan over low heat. Be careful not to burn the garlic. Soften, then cool.
3. In a small bowl, combine milk and bread. Allow bread to soak up milk, then gently squeeze out milk from bread and discard.
4. In a medium bowl, add a slightly beaten egg, meat, cooled onion/ garlic mixture, milk-soaked bread, breadcrumbs, cheese, 3/4 cup ketchup, and a pinch of salt and pepper. Blend together. Don't overmix.
5. Place meatloaf mixture on a baking sheet lined with foil and mold meat into the shape of a loaf of bread.
6. Spread the remaining ketchup on top of meatloaf.
7. Take plastic wrap (yes, plastic wrap) and cover, leaving no air between the wrap and meatloaf. Then cover with foil.
8. Bake in oven 1 hour.
9. Slice and serve warm.

Servings: **8**

Prep Time: **15 minutes**

Cook Time: **1 hour**

SHOPPING LIST

Need
- ☐ Meatloaf mix

May Have on Hand
- ☐ Bread
- ☐ Breadcrumbs
- ☐ Garlic
- ☐ Parsley
- ☐ Onion
- ☐ Parmesan cheese
- ☐ Egg
- ☐ Milk
- ☐ Ketchup
- ☐ Salt and pepper

TIP

You can also make smaller individual loaves of meatloaf and freeze them.

Leftover meatloaf makes a great sandwich.

GRANDMA BARBARA'S BURGERS

My mother never went wrong with her burgers. Serve them straight on a bun or add tons of your favorite toppings. The sky's the limit with Barbara's burgers!

INGREDIENTS

8 ounces Angus ground beef

Toppings:
1 slice beefsteak tomato
2 tablespoons onions, thinly sliced
1 tablespoon shallots, chopped
1 tablespoon vegetable oil
1 slice of cheese
1 slice pickle
3 leaves iceberg lettuce
1 Kaiser roll, lightly toasted
1 tablespoon special sauce
1 tablespoon ketchup
2 slices of crispy bacon

Special sauce:
1 tablespoon mayonnaise
1 tablespoon Worcestershire sauce
Juice of one lemon

DIRECTIONS

1. Form one large burger patty from the ground beef.
2. Place the patty in a very hot skillet or grill pan and cook for 3 - 5 minutes on each side or to your desired cooking temperature. (I prefer a medium rare burger. See the Finger Test on page 255.)
3. Top with cheese while cooking. Let cheese melt then remove the patty and place on a plate. Cover with foil and let rest.
4. Add oil to a small sauté pan over medium heat. Add chopped shallots and sliced onions and cook for 5-10 minutes. Remove and drain on a paper towel.
5. Toast roll.
6. Assemble your burger with the bun, burger, cheese, shallots, onions, and remaining toppings.
7. Combine mayonnaise, Worcestershire sauce and lemon juice to make the special sauce. Can be made ahead of time and refrigerated.
8. Spread the special sauce on bottom bun and squeeze a little ketchup on top bun. Enjoy.

Servings: **1**

Prep Time: **5 minutes**

Cook Time: **10 minutes**

SHOPPING LIST

Need
- ☐ Ground beef
- ☐ Bacon
- ☐ Cheese
- ☐ Lettuce
- ☐ Onions
- ☐ Pickle
- ☐ Shallots
- ☐ Tomato
- ☐ Roll

May Have on Hand
- ☐ Vegetable oil
- ☐ Ketchup
- ☐ Mayonnaise
- ☐ Worscestershire sauce
- ☐ Lemon

AUNT CAROLE'S EVERYDAY CHILI

Most moms have a chili recipe to share. This is a guy's go-to dinner at any age. Everyone loves chili and it's such a versatile meal. You can switch up the meats by using ground chicken, turkey or meatloaf mix.

INGREDIENTS

2 pounds ground beef or any ground meat, cooked and drained
One 15-ounce can tomato sauce
2 medium tomatoes, diced
One 15-ounce can pinto beans (do not drain)
One 15-ounce can kidney beans (do not drain)
2 stalks of celery, chopped
1 cup onion, chopped
1/4 cup enchilada green sauce
2 tablespoons chili powder
1 teaspoon pepper
1 teaspoon salt
2 cups water

Suggested Garnishes

1/2 cup Parmesan, cheddar, or Monterey Jack cheese, grated
2 tablespoons sour cream
Crumbled Saltine crackers or French bread
Guacamole (see recipe on page 11)
Fresh or jarred jalapeno slices

DIRECTIONS

1 In a large pot, brown beef and drain off any fat.

2 Add all ingredients.

3 Cook covered on low heat and simmer for 2 hours. Remember to stir often so the meat doesn't stick to bottom of the pot.

4 Add your preferred garnishes.

5 Serve in a large bowl or on top of baked potato. (See page 237 for baked potato recipe.)

Servings: **6**

Prep Time: **10 minutes**

Cook Time: **3 hours, 10 minutes**

SHOPPING LIST

Need

☐ Celery
☐ Enchilada green sauce
☐ Ground beef
☐ Kidney beans
☐ Onion
☐ Pinto beans
☐ Tomatoes
☐ Tomato sauce

May Have on Hand

☐ Chili powder
☐ Cheese
☐ Sour cream
☐ Saltine crackers
☐ French bread
☐ Guacamole
☐ Jalapenos
☐ Salt and pepper

TIP

Pre-made taco bowls are readily available at any supermarket and make a nice presentation for your chili.

CREMA

8 oz. container sour cream
2 tablespoons heavy cream
2 teaspoons lime juice
Zest of two limes
1 plastic squeeze bottle (Tip: Plastic ketchup or mustard bottles work great. Wash and reuse to dispense your chili crema.)

1. Mix sour cream and heavy cream in a small bowl.

2. Add lime juice and zest to creams.

3. Mix all ingredients then store in a plastic squeeze bottle till ready to serve over chili.

TOPPINGS

3 cups grated cheddar cheese
1/4 cup grated Parmesan cheese
1 medium red onion, chopped
2 sleeves saltine crackers, crushed (Tip: Place the crackers in a large Ziploc bag. Use your hands or a rolling pin to crush them.)

PART 1

INGREDIENTS

1/2 cup unsalted butter
5 pounds ground sirloin
1 pound filet mignon, cut into ¼ inch cubes (save time and ask your butcher to cube the beef for you)
2 cups onion, diced (about 1 large and 2 medium onions)
1 jalapeño, seeds removed and diced
1 bottle Guinness beer
¼ cup flour
32-ounce can, crushed fire roasted tomatoes
1 small can tomato paste
2 32-ounce boxes of beef broth
1 can black beans, drained
1 can kidney beans, drained
½ cup Mexican chili powder
3 tablespoons dark brown sugar
1 teaspoon Kosher salt

DIRECTIONS

1 Melt the butter over medium high heat in a large casserole pot. Sauté meat in butter until browned.

2 With a slotted spoon remove the browned meat and place in a large bowl. Once butter has cooled, use paper towels to soak up 3/4 of the butter, leaving about 2 tablespoons in the pot.

3 Add remaining ingredients into the pot with butter and sauté for 5 minutes. Return meat to the pot. Cook for 30-60 minutes, uncovered. You can eat the chili at this point for a less spicy taste.

KING OF THE HOUSE CHILI

This chili recipe has a slight, but subtle kick. It's thick and made with the finest ingredients. It's the king of all chili, complete with filet and ground sirloin steak.

Great for a crowd or tailgate party. Don't let the ingredients list fool you, this chili is easy to make.

Servings: **12**

Prep Time: **15 minutes**

Cook Time: **3 hours, 10 minutes**

PART 2

INGREDIENTS

4 hot sausages

4 sweet sausages

2 cups onion, diced
(About 1 large and 2 medium onions)

4 tablespoons vegetable oil

1 red pepper, diced

6 garlic cloves, mashed
(Tip: Use the side of a knife to crush and mash the garlic.)

1 jalapeño, seeds removed and diced

2 4-ounce cans green chilies

2 4-ounce cans jalapeño, drained and chopped

4 teaspoons cumin

2 teaspoons cayenne pepper

1 small can RO*TEL tomatoes

2 tablespoons olive oil

1 lime

1 teaspoon Kosher salt

Pepper to taste

DIRECTIONS

1. Over medium heat, sauté onion in oil in a large non-stick pan until translucent, about 10 minutes.

2. Add red pepper, garlic, chilies, jalapeño, cumin, cayenne pepper, and tomatoes to sautéed onion in pan. Sauté for 10 minutes.

3. Preheat oven to 400°F.

4. In a disposable aluminum casserole pan toss hot and sweet sausages with olive oil, Kosher salt and black pepper to taste. Bake for 40 minutes.

5. Remove sausage from the oven. Add sautéed vegetable mixture to aluminum pan with sausage. Bake in oven for 10 minutes.

6. Remove pan from oven. Let cool for 10 minutes, then remove the sausage from pan with tongs. Cut sausages into ½ inch slices. Add vegetable mixture and sausages to casserole pot with chili ingredients from Part 1. Toss, then cook chili over low heat for 35 minutes minimum.

7. Remove from pot and serve in bowls. Top with chopped red onion chopped, fresh cilantro, cheese, lime juice, crackers, and crema. Enjoy.

SHOPPING LIST

Need

- ☐ Sausage (both hot and sweet)
- ☐ Sirloin
- ☐ Filet mignon
- ☐ Cheddar cheese
- ☐ Parmesan cheese
- ☐ Heavy cream
- ☐ Sour cream
- ☐ Onion
- ☐ Red onion
- ☐ Garlic
- ☐ Limes
- ☐ Red pepper
- ☐ Jalapeño
- ☐ Green chilis
- ☐ RO*TEL tomatoes
- ☐ Fire roasted tomatoes
- ☐ Tomato paste
- ☐ Black beans
- ☐ Kidney beans
- ☐ Butter
- ☐ Guiness beer
- ☐ Saltine crackers

May Have on Hand

- ☐ Vegetable oil
- ☐ Olive oil
- ☐ Beef broth
- ☐ Lime
- ☐ Flour
- ☐ Cayenne pepper
- ☐ Cumin
- ☐ Chili powder
- ☐ Dark brown sugar
- ☐ Salt and pepper

COUSIN JAY'S VERSION OF MEMORY POT ROAST

My cousin Jay loves to make his mom's recipes, especially her pot roast. He is the quintessential TASTOSTERONE cook. Jay never strictly follows a recipe and still pleases any hungry crowd with this flavorful meal.

Servings: 4-6

Prep Time: **20 minutes**

Cook Time: **5 hours**

INGREDIENTS

5 pounds of beef bottom round roast
Salt and pepper
2 tablespoons olive oil
4 cups chopped onion
One 15-ounce can chopped tomatoes
1 bay leaf
1 bunch thyme
1 cup white wine
1 cup water
1 pound turnips, peeled and cut into 2-inch slices
1 pound small new potatoes, cut in half
5 carrots, peeled and sliced into 2-inch rounds
1 small package frozen pearl onions
1 small package frozen peas
2 tablespoons parsley, chopped

DIRECTIONS

1. Preheat oven to 300°F.
2. Season beef with salt and pepper.
3. Preheat a large casserole pot over medium heat on stovetop. Add oil and sear seasoned beef for about 10 minutes or until browned on all sides.
4. Add onion, tomatoes, bay leaf, thyme, wine, and water to pot. Bring to a boil, reduce heat and cover. Roast in oven for 3 - 4 hours or insert a meat thermometer into the meat after 3 hours of cooking. At 120° meat is considered rare. This should be your minimum temperature.
5. Remove pot from oven. Add turnips, carrots, and potatoes.
6. Cover and return to oven to cook for an additional 45 minutes.
7. Remove pot from oven. Add frozen peas and pearl onions and cook for 10 additional minutes.
8. Remove meat from pot and cover with foil. Let rest for 10 minutes.
9. Slice into 1/2 inch slices and serve with vegetables. Add parsley as garnish and enjoy.

SHOPPING LIST

Need

☐ Beef roast
☐ Carrots
☐ Onion
☐ Pearl onions
☐ Peas
☐ Potatoes
☐ Parsley (fresh)
☐ Thyme (fresh)
☐ Tomatoes (chopped)
☐ Turnips

May Have on Hand

☐ Bay leaf
☐ Olive oil
☐ White wine
☐ Salt and pepper

PAPA STANLEY'S FILET MIGNON WRAPPED IN BACON

Steak. Need I say more? Bacon. Enough said. This is TASTOSTERONE on a plate. Many families have memories of mom making a nice filet on those special steak nights.

Servings: **2**

Prep Time: **15 minutes**

Cook Time: **10 minutes**

INGREDIENTS

2 pieces of filet mignon

4 slices of bacon

Salt and black pepper

Seasoning salt

1 tablespoon unsalted butter

SHOPPING LIST

Need

☐ Bacon

☐ Filet mignon

May Have on Hand

☐ Butter

☐ Seasoning salt

☐ Salt and pepper

DIRECTIONS

1 Wrap bacon around filet and secure with wooden toothpicks.

2 Season with salt and pepper.

3 Heat grill pan until very hot. Place filets on hot pan for 5 minutes per side or to your desired taste. (I prefer my steak rare and cooked for 3-5 minutes per side.) (See finger test for doneness on page 255.)

4 Remove bacon and continue cooking until crisp.

5 Top with pat of butter, cover with foil and let rest.

6 Slice steaks and serve with crisp bacon.

TIP

All meat should rest prior to cutting. The meat will stay juicy if you have the patience to wait at least a few minutes before serving. Meat will continue to cook after removed from heat.

GLORIA'S CORNED BEEF AND CABBAGE

My cousin's mom Gloria made sure her three sons learned how to cook by preparing meals with them in the kitchen. Thanks to Gloria, her sons love to share their memories of cooking with her and now enjoy cooking with their children.

This recipe is a favorite of her boys - true TASTOSTERONE cooks.

INGREDIENTS

1 pound package of corned beef

Pinch of pickling spice

1 tablespoon salt

2 large onions, peeled

2 lbs potatoes, peeled and cut into thirds

2 large carrots, peeled

1 head cabbage, quartered

Spicy mustard

DIRECTIONS

1 In a large pot add enough water to cover the corned beef.

2 Add onions and pickling spice.

3 Bring to a boil, cover, then simmer for 3 hours. Change water after 1 1/2 hours (optional).

4 Add potatoes to water for the last 30 minutes of cooking.

5 In a separate pot, boil water and add salt.

6 Add carrots and cabbage to boiling water. Cook for 5 minutes then drain.

7 Drain corned beef and potatoes from other pot.

8 Slice corned beef, removing the fat first.

9 Plate with potatoes, carrots, cabbage, and a side of spicy mustard.

Servings: **6**

Prep Time: **5 minutes**

Cook Time: **3 hours**

SHOPPING LIST

Need

☐ Corned beef
☐ Cabbage
☐ Onions
☐ Potatoes
☐ Carrots
☐ Pickling spice

May Have on Hand

☐ Salt
☐ Spicy mustard

TIP

Leftovers from this recipe make great Reuben sandwiches.

Take your corned beef and add sauerkraut, Russian dressing, mayo or mustard, and Swiss cheese on rye bread.

Butter the outsides of your bread; layer the ingredients; and press your sandwich in a panini-maker or on a non-stick pan with a spatula until the cheese starts to melt and the bread is toasted.

DEBBIE'S VEAL ZURICHOISE (SAUTÉED VEAL IN CREAM SAUCE)

On trips to Switzerland my family would indulge in this Swiss family favorite. There are hundreds of ways Swiss mothers make this classic. Here is my twist on the recipe.

INGREDIENTS

1 1/4 pounds boneless veal round or leg, sliced 1/4 inch thick
   and cut into 3 inch strips (ask your butcher to prepare)
3 tablespoons flour
2 tablespoons vegetable oil
3 cups or 1/2 pound white mushrooms, sliced and stems removed
1/3 cup shallots, coarsely chopped
1/2 - 1/3 cup white wine
1/2 cup chicken stock
1/2 cup heavy cream
1/2 cup sour cream
1 tablespoon lemon juice, freshly squeezed
Salt and pepper

DIRECTIONS

1 Season the strips of veal with salt and pepper.
2 Place the flour in a small plastic bag. Add the veal and shake to coat.
3 Heat the oil in a large skillet over medium heat. Add veal and cook over moderate to high heat. Sear veal for about 2 minutes. Center of meat should be pink. Transfer to plate.
4 Add the mushrooms and shallots to skillet. Cook over moderate heat, stirring occasionally until the mushrooms are softened, about 5 minutes. Add the wine and simmer briefly until liquid is absorbed, then add 1/2 cup of chicken stock. Scrape skillet with wooden spoon and cook for an additional 5 minutes.
5 Lower heat and add the heavy cream and sour cream. Simmer over low heat for an additional 5 minutes uncovered.
6 Add veal to skillet and simmer on low heat, being careful not to boil.
7 Add lemon juice and season with salt and pepper.
8 Serve over white rice, shoestring French fries or Swiss Roesti (potato pancakes). (See page 165 for the recipe.)

Servings: 4

Prep Time: **10 minutes**

Cook Time: **15 minutes**

SHOPPING LIST

Need

☐ Veal
☐ Chicken stock
☐ Heavy cream
☐ Sour cream
☐ Mushrooms
☐ Shallots

May Have on Hand

☐ Flour
☐ Lemon
☐ Vegetable oil
☐ White wine
☐ Salt and pepper

SWISS ROESTI
Page 165

GRANDMA SELMA'S CHICKEN IN THE POT

This recipe is my twist on my Grandma Selma's Chicken in the Pot. It's well-worth enjoying at least once a week.

Servings: **4**

Prep Time: **10 minutes**

Cook Time: **20 minutes**

INGREDIENTS

3 tablespoons olive oil
6 large carrots, cut into 3-inch pieces
8 stalks of celery, cut into 3-inch pieces
3 large onions, sliced
Peel of 1 lemon
3 garlic cloves, peeled and mashed
6 sprigs fresh dill
1/2 teaspoon salt
3 pounds chicken breasts, bone-in and skin-on
2 cups low sodium chicken broth
6-8 dumplings or 1/2 package frozen chicken or vegetable pot
   stickers or Chinese dumplings (also known as gyoza.)
Sour cream
Parmesan cheese, grated

DIRECTIONS

1. In a large pot over medium heat, add olive oil.
2. Place all ingredients in the pot (except chicken and pot stickers or dumplings) and sauté for 5 - 10 minutes.
3. Season chicken breasts with salt and pepper. Place chicken in the center of the vegetables.
4. Add broth, enough to almost cover chicken and bring to a boil. Lower heat and simmer covered for 30 - 40 minutes. Vegetables will be al dente. If you prefer softer vegetables, cook for an additional 10 minutes.
5. During the final 3 minutes of cooking, add the frozen pot stickers or dumplings.
6. Remove chicken from the pot and discard the bones and skin.
7. Serve the chicken in a large soup bowl. Ladle the vegetables and pot stickers over the chicken. Sprinkle with fresh dill, grated Parmesan cheese, and a dollop of sour cream.

SHOPPING LIST

Need
- ☐ Chicken breasts
- ☐ Chicken broth
- ☐ Carrots
- ☐ Onions
- ☐ Celery
- ☐ Dill (fresh)
- ☐ Parmesan cheese
- ☐ Sour cream
- ☐ Dumplings or gyoza

May Have on Hand
- ☐ Garlic
- ☐ Lemon
- ☐ Olive oil
- ☐ Salt and pepper

TIP

For a heartier meal, this dish can be served over white rice.

NANA BETTY'S CLASSIC CHICKEN PARMESAN

Classic Chicken Parm is a favorite dish in any house. If you use jarred tomato sauce and prepackaged shredded mozzarella cheese, it's ready in minutes. If you want to go the extra step, you can make your own marinara sauce. Serve this dish with a side of pasta or on Italian bread and it also makes for great leftover sandwiches.

INGREDIENTS

Four 4-ounce skinless, boneless chicken breast halves
2 tablespoons butter
2 tablespoons olive oil
1 1/2 cups of jarred or homemade tomato sauce (see page 247 for recipe)
1 cup flour seasoned with salt and pepper
2 eggs and 1 tablespoon of water mixed together
1 cup seasoned breadcrumbs
1/2 cup Parmesan cheese, grated
1 - 2 cups Mozzarella cheese, shredded (for those who like it more cheesy...
   go for it!)
1 tablespoon fresh basil, chopped
Salt and pepper

DIRECTIONS

1 Preheat oven to 350°F.

2 Season chicken with salt and pepper.

3 Dip chicken into three separate bowls filled with flour, eggs, and breadcrumbs; first coat in flour, then eggs and finally breadcrumbs. (Remember FEB and you'll never forget the easy 3-step process.)

4 Preheat a non-stick frying pan. Add butter and oil.

5 Add chicken and cook for 3 minutes per side until golden brown. Remove with tongs.

6 Drain chicken on paper towels then season with salt and pepper.

7 Place the chicken in an oven safe casserole dish or a disposable aluminum pan. Top with tomato sauce and shredded mozzarella cheese and cover.

8 Bake for 30 minutes.

9 Remove from the oven, top with fresh basil and drizzle with extra virgin olive oil and grated Parmesan cheese. Serve.

Servings: **4**

Prep Time: **10 minutes**

Cook Time: **30 minutes**

SHOPPING LIST

Need

☐ Chicken breasts

☐ Basil (fresh)

☐ Breadcrumbs

☐ Parmesan cheese

☐ Mozzarella cheese

☐ Tomato sauce

May Have on Hand

☐ Eggs

☐ Butter

☐ Flour

☐ Olive oil

☐ Salt and pepper

TOMATO SAUCE
Page 247

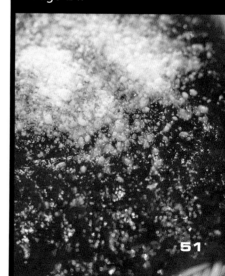

GRANDMA'S CHICKEN AND CREAM SAUCE

Cream and butter have a way of melting the heart. This is another family favorite recipe that will make its way to your table in a matter of minutes.

INGREDIENTS

Four 4-ounce skinless, boneless chicken breast halves, cut into 3" x 1" strips (ask your butcher to prepare)
1 tablespoon olive oil
1 tablespoon butter
1/2 teaspoon salt
1/4 teaspoon pepper
1/2 cup shallots, chopped or 1 small yellow onion, finely diced
1/4 cup white wine (today's boxed wines are terrific and they last for weeks)
3/4 cup low sodium canned chicken broth or my "Worth it Chicken Stock" (see page 29 for recipe)
1/3 cup heavy cream
3 tablespoons fresh parsley sprigs, chopped
1 tablespoon fresh tarragon, chopped (optional)

DIRECTIONS

1. Preheat large sauté pan over medium heat. Add oil and butter.
2. Season the chicken with salt and pepper. Add the chicken to the pan, shaking pan often so it does not stick. Cook chicken 3 - 5 minutes until no longer pink on the inside. Cut a small slit inside the chicken to test for pinkness.
3. Remove chicken from pan with slotted spoon or tongs. Set aside on a plate.
4. Add shallots or onions to the same pan. Add more oil if needed to sauté the vegetables.
5. Using a wooden spoon, scrape the chicken bits and shallots or onions so they cook evenly.
6. Add white wine and turn heat to high. As wine cooks, continue to scrape the bits of the chicken and vegetables with the spoon from the bottom of the pan. Wine will reduce as you cook. Cook until wine reduces in half, about 2 minutes.
7. Add chicken stock and cook for 3 additional minutes.
8. Reduce heat. Add cream and fresh herbs and cook for 3 additional minutes.
9. Add chicken and juices to pan. Cook until chicken is coated with sauce and warmed through.
10. Add salt and pepper to taste and garnish with chopped parsley and tarragon (optional).
11. Serve over rice and make sure to sop up all that great sauce with a piece of crusty bread.

Servings: **4**

Prep Time: **10 minutes**

Cook Time: **15 minutes**

SHOPPING LIST

Need

☐ Chicken breasts

☐ Chicken broth

☐ Heavy cream

☐ Parsley

☐ Shallot or onion

May Have on Hand

☐ Butter

☐ Olive oil

☐ White wine

☐ Salt and pepper

Optional

☐ Tarragon

WORTH IT CHICKEN STOCK Page 29

SAMANTHA'S SHRIMP SCAMPI WITH PARMESAN

My daughter Samantha often requests this dish, which has just the right mix of creamy sweet goodness and garlic.

INGREDIENTS

1 cup olive oil

4 lemons, 3 juiced, 1 whole

1/2 cup white wine

6 garlic cloves, minced

1/2 cup fresh parsley, chopped

5 tablespoons unsalted butter (reserve 2 tablespoons for topping)

3 teaspoons sweet paprika

1/2 teaspoon salt

1/2 teaspoon black pepper

2 pounds shrimp, cleaned and deveined (if buying fresh, ask your fishmonger how to clean and devein shrimp or buy frozen and thaw according to directions)

1 cup seasoned breadcrumbs

1/4 cup Parmigiano-Reggiano cheese, grated

DIRECTIONS

1 Preheat oven to 350°F.

2 In a large sauté pan, combine all ingredients except for the shrimp, breadcrumbs, cheese, and 2 tablespoons of butter. Heat for 5 minutes then cool.

3 Pour mixture into an oven safe glass baking dish. Add the shrimp then top with breadcrumbs and cheese.

4 Cut up remaining butter and place onto breadcrumbs.

5 Bake covered in oven for 10 - 15 minutes. Uncover, then place in broiler for 5 additional minutes.

6 Remove when crust browns, then squeeze lemon on top and serve.

Servings: **4-6**

Prep Time: **10 minutes**

Cook Time: **20 minutes**

SHOPPING LIST

Need

☐ Shrimp

☐ Lemons

☐ Parsley (fresh)

☐ Breadcrumbs

☐ Parmigiano-Reggiano cheese

May Have on Hand

☐ Garlic

☐ Sweet paprika

☐ Olive oil

☐ Butter

☐ White wine

☐ Salt and pepper

AUNT ZUZU'S FISH TACO

This dish is so refreshing and doubly delicious with an ice-cold beer on a hot summer day. Don't flounder around anymore with other recipes because this is the perfect fish taco dish.

INGREDIENTS

1 pound flounder fillet or any white flaky fish

1 cup vegetable oil

1 cup flour, seasoned with salt and pepper (1/2 teaspoon of each)

1 tablespoon Old Bay seasoning

1/4 cup tomatoes, chopped

1/4 cup red onion, chopped

1 avocado, sliced

1/4 cup iceberg lettuce, shredded

6 soft tortillas

Sauce

1 tablespoon tartar sauce

1 tablespoon salsa

DIRECTIONS

1. On a large plate, combine flour, Old Bay seasoning, salt and pepper. Dip fish in water and coat with flour and seasonings.

2. In a large sauté pan, heat oil over medium heat until hot. Place fish in pan and fry for 3 minutes per side. Turn with tongs. Remove from heat and place on paper towels.

3. In same oil, fry the tortillas for 2 minutes per side until brown. Remove from heat and dry on paper towels.

4. Combine tartar sauce and salsa in a small bowl to make sauce.

5. Fill tortillas with fish, onion, lettuce, avocado, tomatoes, and sauce and serve.

Servings: **4**

Prep Time: **10 minutes**

Cook Time: **10 minutes**

SHOPPING LIST

Need
- [ ] Fish
- [ ] Avocado
- [ ] Tomatoes
- [ ] Red onion
- [ ] Lettuce
- [ ] Old Bay seasoning
- [ ] Salsa
- [ ] Tartar sauce
- [ ] Tortillas

May Have on Hand
- [ ] Flour
- [ ] Vegetable oil
- [ ] Salt and pepper

TIPS

You can test if the oil in a pan is hot by sticking the handle of a wooden spoon into the pan. If oil bubbles around the handle then the oil is hot and ready for cooking.

Cooking supply stores sell splatter screens, which are used to cover your pan while cooking so oil does not harm you or get all over your kitchen.

DEBRA'S BEST BOLOGNESE

If you think Bolognese is difficult to prepare or heavy on the stomach, think again with this classic recipe. When preparing this dish, I often freeze a few containers for dinner the following week.

INGREDIENTS

5 carrots, peeled and diced
5 celery ribs, diced
1 large onion, chopped
3 tablespoons olive oil
1 garlic clove, minced
Pinch of red pepper flakes
2 pounds ground veal, chicken or beef
2 small cans of tomato paste
3 tablespoons flour
1/2 cup white wine
1 quart chicken stock or canned chicken broth
A small bundle of fresh thyme, parsley and oregano
    tied together with cooking string
1/2 cup ricotta cheese
1/2 cup of Parmesan cheese, grated
2 tablespoons parsley, chopped
Box of pasta
Salt and black pepper

DIRECTIONS

1. Preheat large sauté pan over medium to high heat for two minutes.
2. Add oil and heat for one minute.
3. Add vegetables, garlic, salt, pepper and red pepper flakes to pan.
4. Sauté over medium heat for 10 minutes or until vegetables soften.
5. Brown meat in another pan over medium heat. Do not add oil as the fat will cook the meat.
6. Add meat to vegetables.
7. Add flour to mixture and cook over medium heat for one minute.
8. Add one can of tomato paste. The mixture will look dry at this point. Cook for one minute.
9. Add wine and cook for 2 minutes.
10. Add chicken stock and fresh herbs. Bring to a boil, then lower heat and simmer uncovered for 30 minutes. Stir occasionally to make sure the meat doesn't stick to the pan.
11. Add second can of paste and cook for an additional 30 minutes.
12. Remove herbs and discard.
13. Boil large pot of water with a pinch of salt. Add your pasta of choice and cook per directions on the packaging. To cook al dente pasta, take about two minutes off the cooking time.
14. Spoon Bolognese over cooked pasta. Sprinkle with grated Parmesan cheese, chopped parsley, and a dollop of ricotta cheese.

Servings: **6**

Prep Time: **15 minutes**

Cook Time: **1 hour, 20 minutes**

SHOPPING LIST

Need
- ☐ Meat
- ☐ Chicken stock
- ☐ Carrots
- ☐ Celery
- ☐ Onion
- ☐ Oregano
- ☐ Parsley
- ☐ Thyme
- ☐ Parmesan cheese
- ☐ Ricotta cheese
- ☐ Tomato paste
- ☐ Pasta

May Have on Hand
- ☐ Olive oil
- ☐ Flour
- ☐ Garlic
- ☐ Red pepper flakes
- ☐ White wine
- ☐ Salt and pepper

TIP

To save time, buy packaged precut vegetables.

GREAT GRANDMA'S HUNGARIAN GOULASH

Luckily, my Hungarian ancestors brought this family favorite to Ellis Island. This dish is warm, hearty and satisfies any hungry crowd.

INGREDIENTS

1/4 cup vegetable oil
1 large yellow onion, chopped
1 clove garlic, minced
3 tablespoons sweet paprika
3 pounds beef chunks for stew, cut into large 3 inch cubes
One 26-ounce can chopped tomatoes
2 green peppers, cut into 1/2-inch cubes
1 teaspoon caraway seeds
1/2 teaspoon salt
1/4 teaspoon black pepper
4 cups low-sodium beef broth
1 pound small potatoes
5 sprigs fresh marjoram or tarragon, chopped
1/2 cup frozen peas (optional)
1/2 cup frozen pearl onions (optional)
3/4 cup chopped green cabbage (optional)
2 tablespoons heavy cream or sour cream (optional)
One-pound bag of butter egg noodles

DIRECTIONS

1   In a very large soup pot, heat oil over medium heat.
2   Add onion and garlic, then lower heat.
3   Add paprika.
4   Add beef, tomatoes, pepper, caraway seeds, salt, pepper, and broth.
5   Bring to a boil. Lower heat, cover, and simmer for 2 hours.
6   Add potato and herbs. Cover, then simmer for 35 minutes or until potatoes are soft.
7   Add the optional ingredients now. Cook for 5 additional minutes.
8   Garnish with fresh herbs (marjoram or tarragon) and serve over butter egg noodles.

Servings: **8**

Prep Time: **25 minutes**

Cook Time: **3 hours**

SHOPPING LIST

Need
☐ Beef broth
☐ Beef chunks
☐ Garlic
☐ Marjoram or tarragon
☐ Yellow onion
☐ Green peppers
☐ Potatoes
☐ Tomatoes (crushed)
☐ Egg noodles

May Have on Hand
☐ Vegetable oil
☐ Caraway seeds
☐ Sweet paprika
☐ Salt and pepper

Optional
☐ Cabbage
☐ Pearl onions
☐ Peas
☐ Heavy cream

TIP

To make into a great soup, add 10 cups beef broth.

MAMA MEL'S BEST LASAGNA

Carmella, known as Mama Mel, worked at my family's car dealership for years. She would serve this lasagna dish to the enjoyment of friends and family for years. It's a time consuming dish, but well worth the effort. If you omit the meat, this recipe is just as delicious and quicker to prepare. It's rated a Triple-T because it does take some tools, technique and time to make this TASTOSTERONE recipe.

Servings: 10+

Prep Time: 50 minutes

Cook Time: 3 hours

INGREDIENTS

Two 24-ounce cans of tomato puree
One 24-ounce can crushed tomatoes
One 6-ounce can of tomato paste
2 tablespoons olive oil
2 eggs
1 garlic clove, peeled and mashed
1 tablespoon garlic, minced
1-1/2 pounds sweet sausage, casing removed and shaped into 1-inch patties
1-1/2 pounds hot sausage, casing removed and shaped into 1-inch patties
1-1/2 pounds mixture of ground pork and beef, shaped into 1-inch patties
1 pound mozzarella cheese, coarsely shredded
1 pound ricotta cheese
1/2 cup Parmigiano-Reggiano cheese, grated
1/2 cup Italian parsley, coarsely chopped
1/4 cup breadcrumbs
1/2 cup water
1/2 cup Marsala wine
1 pound package of curly lasagna noodles
Salt and pepper

SHOPPING LIST

Need
- [ ] Ground pork and beef
- [ ] Sausage (sweet)
- [ ] Sausage (hot)
- [ ] Eggs
- [ ] Mozzarella cheese
- [ ] Parmigiano-Reggiano cheese
- [ ] Ricotta cheese
- [ ] Parsley (fresh Italian)
- [ ] Lasagna noodles
- [ ] Tomato puree
- [ ] Tomatoes (crushed)
- [ ] Tomato paste

May Have on Hand
- [ ] Breadcrumbs
- [ ] Garlic
- [ ] Olive oil
- [ ] Marsala wine
- [ ] Salt and pepper

DIRECTIONS

1. In a large pot, heat 3 tablespoons of olive oil over medium-low heat and sauté garlic for 2 minutes to flavor the oil. Discard garlic after cooking.
2. Add all cans of tomatoes to pot and bring to a boil. Lower heat and simmer.
3. In a pan, sauté the sausage over medium heat until brown for about 3 minutes per side.
4. Add the cooked sausage to the pot with tomatoes then cook uncovered over low heat until the sauce simmers for 30 - 40 minutes. Small bubbles will form.
5. Add water and Marsala wine to the pot of cooked sausage and tomato sauce. Bring to a boil over high heat, then lower heat and simmer for an additional hour.
6. Place the ground pork and beef in a bowl. Mix eggs, 1/3 cup Parmigiano-Reggiano, minced garlic, breadcrumbs, salt, and pepper to the meat mixture. Combine ingredients well then shape into large meatballs.
7. In the pan used to cook the sausage, over medium heat add the meatballs and brown. Add the meatballs to the sauce that has been cooking and simmer uncovered for an additional hour.
8. Add meatballs and simmer covered for an additional hour.
9. In a large pot, filled halfway with water add about a teaspoon of salt. Bring water to a boil.
10. Add curly lasagna noodles to the large pot. Boiling water for 4 minutes, then drain.
11. Remove the sausage and meatballs from the sauce with a large slotted spoon. Let cool. Mash the meats together in a bowl.
12. Coat the bottom of a large casserole dish with sauce then layer with cooked pasta, then meat, then sauce, then ricotta, and then mozzarella. Repeat. The top layer should be pasta, sauce, mozzarella, and Parmigiano-Reggiano cheese.
13. Cover with foil and bake in a preheated oven set to 350ºF. Bake 40 - 60 minutes or until sauce is bubbling, uncover for the last 5 minutes to brown the top layer of lasagna.
14. Remove from oven and cool for 30 minutes before serving.

LOBSTERS ON THE INSIDE GRILL
Page 81

SWISS FONDUE
Page 67

CHICKEN MARSALA MAGIC Page 91

I WANT MUSSELS
Page 77

GRAVALAX AND TOAST Page 73

CHAPTER 3

"DINNER, DARLING"

You're exhausted and arrive home from work, quickly crashing into your favorite chair to watch some TV. Starving, you smell dinner coming from the kitchen. Then you hear the words, "Dinner, darling!" and are called to enjoy a mouthwatering home cooked meal.

Except, no longer are you the one on the chair waiting for dinner. You're now the cook, and there is nothing sweeter than a strong, male voice coming from the kitchen.

TASTOSTERONE is served and so is your new confidence thanks to the tools and recipes in TASTOSTERONE: The Best Cookbook for Men. Any man can make a reservation for dinner, but a chef with TASTOSTERONE wows everyone by heating things up in the kitchen. There is nothing sexier than a man slicing and dicing away, while cooking up a romantic feast. The recipes in this chapter take no time at all to make and a recipe like my "Florida Stone Crabs" doesn't even require cooking - just a great fishmonger, a mallet, some mustard, mayo, and a crisp chardonnay.

SWISS FONDUE

When I visit Switzerland I make it a point to stop in the village of Gruyère for fondue. After a long day of skiing, there is nothing more indulgent than huddling around this simple Swiss treat in a pot that requires only a few quality ingredients to warm up the day. In Switzerland, there are no fancy fondues with mixings of salsa and cheddar cheese; instead, they use only the best bread and Gruyère cheese available to make this simple meal. The Swiss do however have terms and conditions for eating this amazing dish; don't drop your bread into the fondue or you will end up in the nearby lake and don't drink water or anything carbonated while eating fondue. One should drink a white wine such as Fendant or hot tea, otherwise you'll end up with cheese balls that will wreak havoc in your stomach.

INGREDIENTS

Fondue pot and forks (I own a Calphalon Stainless Steel Fondue set
   and have used it for years. It's a great product; well worth the investment.)
1 garlic clove, chopped
3-4 cups Gruyère cheese, shredded
2 tablespoons cornstarch
1/2 - 3/4 cup dry white wine/Fendant (see Tips)
1 lemon
2 tablespoons Kirsch (clear-colored, cherry-flavored brandy/liquor)
Fresh ground pepper
French bread
Cornishon or any small-sized pickles
Pickled onions

DIRECTIONS

1 Warm the fondue pot on a low flame. (Follow cooking directions for your fondue maker.)

2 Toss cheese and cornstarch. Set aside.

3 Rub garlic on all sides inside the pot for flavor then discard garlic.

4 Add the dry white wine (Fendant) and a squeeze of lemon. Heat till warm.

5 Add cheese and cornstarch, then stir.

6 Add Kirsch and continue to stir. At this point, the fondue should have a glossy shine. Continue to stir in pot over flame.

7 Grind fresh pepper on the cheese as it comes out of pot.

8 Serve with crusty bread, cut into 2 inch cubes.

9 Dip bread into fondue and serve with Cornishon pickles and pearl onions on the side.

Servings: **4**

Prep Time: **10 minutes**

Cook Time: **5 minutes**

SHOPPING LIST

Need
- ☐ Gruyère cheese
- ☐ Bread
- ☐ Cornishon pickles
- ☐ Garlic
- ☐ Picked onions
- ☐ Wine (dry, white) or Fendant
- ☐ Kirsch
- ☐ Fondue port and forks

May Have on Hand
- ☐ Cornstarch
- ☐ Lemon
- ☐ Pepper

TIPS

A Swiss Fendant is a white dry wine that goes well with fondue. Fondue cheeses are most commonly melted in a dry white wine to help keep the cheese from the direct heat as it melts. It also adds flavor. Use the wine and avoid cheese balls at your party!

THE GOOD STUFF

This is the perfect dinner for your little darlings. When "The Good Stuff" is served, not a morsel will be left on your children's plates. I would recommend having these ingredients in your pantry for a quick dinner.

INGREDIENTS

1 pound ground beef

1 small can bamboo shoots, drained

One 11-ounce can of bean sprouts, drained

A pinch of powdered ginger

1/2 cup soy sauce

1/2 cup water

Splash of white wine

White rice

Oriental noodles (optional)

DIRECTIONS

1. Sauté meat in pan over medium heat until no longer pink. Tilting pan over sink, drain fat while meat stays in the pan.

2. Add the remaining ingredients and heat for 5 additional minutes.

3. Serve over steaming white rice and top with crunchy Oriental noodles.

Servings: **4**

Prep Time: **5 minutes**

Cook Time: **5 minutes**

SHOPPING LIST

Need

☐ Ground beef

☐ Bamboo shoots

☐ Bean sprouts

May Have on Hand

☐ White rice

☐ Powdered ginger

☐ Soy sauce

☐ White wine

Optional

☐ Oriental noodles

HOW TO COOK RICE
Page 243

THE UGLY STUFF

My daughter Samantha and I were watching the Food Network's "The Best Thing I Ever Ate" one evening and the chef described enjoying the ugliest dish he had ever seen.

Despite it's appearance, we were immediately inspired to create our own version of what we now call "The Ugly Stuff". And there is nothing ugly about how amazing this dish tastes!

INGREDIENTS

1 large onion, chopped

1 tablespoon vegetable oil

1 1/2 pounds ground beef

10-ounce box frozen chopped or leaf spinach, defrosted and drained
(Be sure to squeeze out excess water.)

2 eggs

Salt and pepper

1/4 cup Parmesan cheese (optional)

DIRECTIONS

1 Heat oil in a medium sauté pan. Add onions and cook over medium heat until brown, about 5 minutes.

2 Add meat. Cook and stir until meat browns for an additional 5 minutes.

3 Add spinach, salt and pepper to pan. Combine and cook an additional minute.

4 Crack open eggs, add to pan and cook an additional minute.

5 Sprinkle with Parmesan cheese then mix again. Serve.

Servings: **4**

Prep Time: **10 minutes**

Cook Time: **15 minutes**

SHOPPING LIST

Need

☐ Ground beef

☐ Eggs

☐ Onion

☐ Spinach

May Have on Hand

☐ Vegetable oil

☐ Salt and pepper

Optional

☐ Parmesan cheese

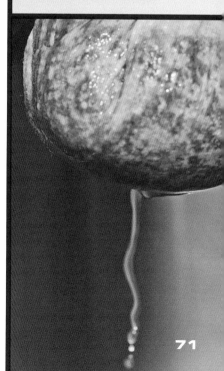

GRAVLAX AND TOAST

The word gravlax comes from the Scandinavian word grav, which means "grave" or "hole in the ground" and lax (or laks), which means "salmon", thus gravlax means "buried salmon". An easy way to remember this recipe is when you're buried in work at the office, you can still come home, whip up this dish and enjoy a romantic evening with your wife.

INGREDIENTS

1/2 pound gravlax cured in dill, thinly sliced
6 slices bread
2 hard-boiled eggs (chop yolks and whites separately)
3 tablespoons red onion, minced
3 tablespoons capers, drained
1 1/4 cup frisée, watercress or lettuce
3 lemons, cut into wedges
2 tablespoons fresh dill, chopped
3 tablespoons unsalted butter

Mustard Sauce
1 tablespoon sugar
1 teaspoon white wine vinegar
5 tablespoons yellow mustard
5 tablespoons olive oil
1 teaspoon fresh dill, chopped
1 teaspoon créme fraiche or sour cream

DIRECTIONS

Mustard Sauce

Whisk together ingredients and serve with gravlax.

How to plate gravlax for serving:

1 On a large serving plate, place all ingredients in separate piles with the gravlax in the center.
2 Toast bread.
3 Top a slice of bread with gravlax and any of your favorite toppings and sauce.

Servings: 4

Prep Time: 5 minutes

Cook Time: None

SHOPPING LIST

Need
☐ Gravlax
☐ Eggs
☐ Capers
☐ Créme fraiche or sour cream
☐ Frisée, watercress or lettuce
☐ Red onion
☐ Dill (fresh)
☐ Lemons

May Have on Hand
☐ Butter
☐ Mustard
☐ Olive oil
☐ Sugar
☐ White wine vinegar
☐ Bread

FRIEND OR FOIE

Foie Gras is a dish for the adventurous man, but I promise you won't have to scale mountains to find the ingredients. You can also impress your date by throwing in a sexy French accent, green salad, bread, a wedge of your favorite cheese and champagne.

Servings: **2**

Prep Time: **10 minutes**

Cook Time: **6 minutes**

INGREDIENTS

1/4 cup yellow raisins

1 tablespoon capers, drained

3 tablespoons Madeira wine or sherry

1/4 cup chicken stock or broth

Two 1-inch thick slices duck foie gras, fresh or frozen

DIRECTIONS

1. Combine raisins, capers and wine in a small bowl. Set aside.

2. Preheat small sauté or grill pan over medium heat.

3. Sear duck foie gras in pan for 2 minutes per side till browned. Remove foie gras with slotted spoon, leaving any juices rendered in pan.

4. Add raisin mixture to pan over low heat and cook for two minutes, stirring frequently.

5. Pour over duck foie gras and serve immediately with crusty bread.

SHOPPING LIST

Need

☐ Foie gras

☐ Chicken stock

☐ Capers

☐ Madiera wine or sherry

☐ Yellow raisins

TIPS

Top a burger or steak with foie gras for a trendy new twist on the dish.

Duck foie gras can be found in your gourmet grocer's freezer.

I WANT MUSSELS

You don't need to hit the gym to show off these mussels. This recipe makes the perfect appetizer or starter to any romantic meal.

Servings: **4**

Prep Time: **5 minutes**

Cook Time: **5 minutes**

INGREDIENTS

3-4 pounds mussels

1 cup onions, chopped

2 tablespoons shallots, coarsely chopped

1 tablespoon unsalted butter

2 bay leaves

5 tablespoons Italian parsley, coarsely chopped

1/2 teaspoon pepper

1 1/2 cups white wine or dry white vermouth

SHOPPING LIST

Need

☐ Mussels

☐ Onions

☐ Italian Parsley

☐ Shallots

☐ White wine or vermouth

May Have on Hand

☐ Butter

☐ Bay leaves

☐ Pepper

DIRECTIONS

1. Place the mussels, onions, shallots, butter, bay leaves, parsley, and pepper in a large casserole pot with lid. Toss the ingredients then pour white wine or vermouth over mixture and cover.

2. Bring to a boil for 2-5 minutes then shake pan to prevent anything from sticking to the bottom.

3. Peek into your pot. If most of the mussels are open, pour them onto a large serving plate and garnish with chopped parsley. Discard any unopened mussels.

4. Serve with crusty bread.

TIPS

To clean mussels, clams or oysters, place them in a strainer in your sink.

I use my sink spray gun to wash them, but if you don't have one run them under cold water and scrub with a clean sponge.

After cooking, make sure to discard any unopened mussels before serving.

FLORIDA STONE CRABS

Joe's Stone Crab Restaurant in Miami Beach made these gems of the ocean famous. No need to hop on a plane, this delicacy in now readily available at your local seafood market.

Servings: 2

Prep Time: **5 minutes**

Cook Time: **None**

INGREDIENTS

3 pounds Florida stone crab claws, cracked and chilled

Mustard Dip

1/4 cup mayonnaise

3 tablespoons Dijon-style mustard
  (for the mustard fan, add more if needed)

DIRECTIONS

1 Mix together mayonnaise and mustard for dressing.

2 Place the chilled crab claws on a large serving plate.

3 Serve with mustard sauce, lobster crackers and small forks.

TIPS

Stone crab season runs from October 15th till May 15th.

Ask your fishmonger to crack the claws for you to save on preparation time.

Stone crab claws do not require cooking because they are cooked when harvested.

SHOPPING LIST

Need

☐ Stone crab claws

May Have on Hand

☐ Mayonnaise

☐ Mustard

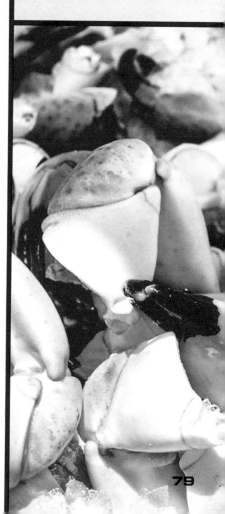

LOBSTERS ON THE INSIDE GRILL

Spoil your partner by presenting her with the best shellfish the sea has to offer.

Lobster has long been a luxury dish so cooking it is a no brainer for the man looking to make the perfect romantic meal.

INGREDIENTS

4 Maine or Brazilian lobster tails, split in half (Maine lobsters are typically sweeter and smaller. These can be found in the frozen section of your grocer.)

2 tablespoons olive oil

3/4 stick butter

1 lemon

Salt and pepper

DIRECTIONS

1 Preheat grill pan over high heat.

2 Season lobster tails with salt and pepper to taste. Brush them with oil.

3 Place lobster tails, meat side down, directly on grill to sear. The shell should not touch the grill. Cook for 5 minutes.

4 Remove the lobsters from the grill, meat side up, and brush with a little more oil. Cover with foil.

5 In a small sauté pan over low heat melt the butter.

6 Spoon some butter over lobsters. Serve with lemon wedge.

Servings: **4**

Prep Time: **5 minutes**

Cook Time: **10 minutes**

SHOPPING LIST

Need

☐ Lobster

☐ Lemon

May Have on Hand

☐ Olive oil

☐ Butter

☐ Salt and pepper

HEART AND "SOLE" (GRAY SOLE ALMONDINE)

Gray sole is a fish that has a mild flavor and not many bones. It has a nice, light and flaky consistency that is perfect for the person apprehensive about the "fishy" taste associated with seafood.

INGREDIENTS

Four 4-ounce filets of gray sole (or any other type of sole)

2 eggs, lightly beaten with 1 tablespoon of water (egg wash)

2 cups seasoned breadcrumbs

4 tablespoons unsalted butter

2 tablespoons olive oil

1/2 cup toasted white slivered almonds

1 lemon

Salt and pepper

2 tablespoons parsley (optional)

DIRECTIONS

1 Dip fish in egg and water mixture then coat with breadcrumbs.

2 Preheat 2 tablespoons of butter and oil in a sauté pan over medium heat.

3 Sauté the fish for 3 minutes per side until golden brown. Set aside on a plate lined with paper towel. Season with salt and pepper to taste.

4 Add 2 tablespoons of butter and the juice of one lemon to sauté pan.

5 Toast almonds in a separate small, non-stick sauté pan over medium heat. Watch them closely as they only require 1 - 2 minutes to cook until done. Add toasted almonds to pan with lemon and butter and cook for 2 minutes.

6 Place fish in an ovenproof pan. Pour almond mixture over fish and broil for 1 minute.

7 Garnish with chopped parsley (optional.)

Servings: **4**

Prep Time: **10 minutes**

Cook Time: **10 minutes**

SHOPPING LIST

Need

☐ Sole filets

☐ Butter

☐ Eggs

☐ Almonds

☐ Breadcrumbs

☐ Lemon

May Have on Hand

☐ Olive oil

☐ Salt and pepper

Optional

☐ Parsley

RACK UP THE LAMB

The game is on! Rack of lamb is a tender dish that will help rack up the brownie points in any relationship.

Servings: **2**

Prep Time: **10 minutes**

Cook Time: **45 minutes**

INGREDIENTS

1 rack of lamb (American or New Zealand)

1 garlic clove, thinly sliced

2-3 tablespoons Dijon-style mustard

1 cup seasoned breadcrumbs

1/2 cup Parmigiano-Reggiano cheese, grated

3 tablespoons olive oil

1 tablespoon unsalted butter

SHOPPING LIST

Need
- ☐ Rack of lamb
- ☐ Parmigiano-Reggiano cheese
- ☐ Breadcrumbs

May Have on Hand
- ☐ Butter
- ☐ Olive oil
- ☐ Mustard
- ☐ Garlic

DIRECTIONS

1. Preheat oven to 350°F.
2. Line a baking sheet with non-stick foil.
3. Season lamb with salt and pepper.
4. Using a small sharp knife, cut small slits into the top of the lamb. Place the garlic slices into the slits.
5. Spread mustard over the entire rack of lamb.
6. In a separate bowl, mix together breadcrumbs, parsley and cheese. Coat rack of lamb with mixture, pressing it into the mustard.
7. Drizzle olive oil on top of breadcrumb mixture.
8. Top lamb with pats of butter.
9. Place lamb on baking sheet. Cook for 30 - 45 minutes depending on how you prefer your meat done.
10. Remove from oven. Let meat rest for 15 minutes then cut into 2 sections.

TIP

If you prefer a less gamey taste, soak your lamb chops in milk for a maximum of two hours and refrigerate until you are ready to cook. Rinse off and pat dry before proceeding with recipe.

FOR THE LOVE OF LAMB

For the love of your family, make this hearty meal of orzo and lamb. It's sure to please the wife and kids and earn you notches up the T-Man totem pole. This is a great dish to make ahead so you can spend more time with your family or friends and less time in the kitchen.

INGREDIENTS

4 tablespoons olive oil (reserve 2 tablespoons for Step 6)
1 pound lamb stew meat or 2 pounds lamb shoulder, sliced into 3 inch slices/cubes
4 tablespoons unsalted butter
1 cup onion, finely chopped
1 tablespoon garlic, chopped
1 cup white wine
1 1/2 cups orzo
6 cups low sodium chicken stock or broth
1 jar of roasted red peppers, drained and chopped
1/4 cup fresh Italian parsley, chopped
1/2 cup Parmesan or Asiago cheese, shredded
Salt and pepper
2 lemons, cut into wedges (optional)

DIRECTIONS

1 Preheat large saute pan over medium heat. Add oil.

2 Season lamb with salt and pepper and add to hot oil. Sauté for 2 minutes then remove lamb and set aside. After the pan cools, wipe clean with paper towels.

3 In same pan, over medium, add 2 tablespoons butter. Once hot, add onion and garlic. Cook for 2 minutes. Add cooked lamb and wine. Cook for 4 minutes.

4 Over low heat stir in uncooked orzo. Add 2 cups of warmed broth (see tip) and stir until reduced, 10-15 minutes. Do not stop stirring or pasta will stick and burn. Continue to add broth, 2 cups at a time, reducing between each addition, until all broth is incorporated. Each time broth is added the cooking time to reduce liquid can take up to 15 additional minutes. Do not stop stirring.

5 Remove pan from heat once all broth has been reduced.

6 Add remaining 2 tablespoons of butter, red peppers, parsley, and salt.

7 Mix in the cheese and top with parsley, salt, and pepper to taste.

8 Serve with lemon wedges and garnish with parsley.

Servings: **4**

Prep Time: **15 minutes**

Cook Time: **40 minutes**

SHOPPING LIST

Need
☐ Lamb
☐ Chicken stock
☐ Garlic
☐ Lemons
☐ Onion
☐ Roasted red peppers
☐ Parsley
☐ Orzo
☐ Parmesan or Asiago cheese
☐ White wine

May Have on Hand
☐ Olive oil
☐ Butter
☐ Salt and pepper

TIP

Save time and cleanup by placing broth in a large 1-quart Pyrex measuring cup and heating the broth in the microwave.

VEAL MILANESE

Veal is a tender meat that can be pretty versatile. I sometimes add chopped arugula salad or bruschetta to this dish for variety. (See recipes for Arugula Salad on page 149 and Bruschetta on page 151.)

INGREDIENTS

1 pound veal chops, thinly pounded with bone attached
  (Your butcher can do this step for you.)

2 eggs, slightly beaten

1 cup flour seasoned with salt and pepper

1/4 cup Parmesan cheese, grated

3/4 cup seasoned breadcrumbs

2 tablespoons fresh Italian parsley, chopped

1 teaspoon dried oregano

2 tablespoons olive oil

2 tablespoons unsalted butter

DIRECTIONS

1. Create your FEB: place flour in a bowl and season with salt and pepper. In another bowl, create an egg wash by adding one lightly beaten egg to water. Season with salt and pepper. Place breadcrumbs and Parmesan cheese in a third bowl. Toss to combine.

2. Season veal with salt and pepper and dip in flour, then egg, followed by breadcrumbs.

3. Preheat oil and butter in a large sauté pan over medium heat.

4. Place veal in pan and cook for 3 minutes per side until golden brown.

5. Remove veal from the oil and flavor with lemon juice, salt and pepper. Serve with arugula salad or bruschetta.

Servings: **4**

Prep Time: **10 minutes**

Cook Time: **10 minutes**

SHOPPING LIST

Need

☐ Veal

☐ Eggs

☐ Parmesan cheese

☐ Parsley

☐ Breadcrumbs

May Have on Hand

☐ Butter

☐ Olive oil

☐ Oregano

☐ Flour

☐ Salt and pepper

ARUGULA SALAD
Page 149

CHICKEN MARSALA MAGIC

For new parents experiencing sleepless nights, this dish makes it possible to prepare something delicious and quick. You don't have to wait until a special occasion to make this meal and it can even make a groggy night something romantic.

Servings: 4

Prep Time: 20 minutes

Cook Time: 20 minutes

INGREDIENTS

Four 4-ounce boneless, skinless (optional) chicken breast halves
  (Your butcher can do this for you.)
3 tablespoons flour seasoned with salt and pepper
3 tablespoons olive oil
4 tablespoons butter
1/2 pound white mushrooms, cleaned, stems removed, and sliced
1/2 cup Marsala wine
1/2 cup chicken stock or broth
3 tablespoons fresh parsley, chopped
Salt and pepper

SHOPPING LIST

Need

☐ Chicken breasts
☐ Chicken stock or broth
☐ Mushrooms
☐ Parsley (fresh)
☐ Marsala wine

May Have on Hand

☐ Butter
☐ Flour
☐ Olive oil
☐ Salt and pepper

DIRECTIONS

1. Place flour in a plastic bag and season with salt and pepper.
2. Coat chicken with flour and shake off excess.
3. Preheat sauté pan over medium heat. Add oil and 2 tablespoons butter to the pan.
4. Place chicken in pan and cook for 4 minutes per side. Don't overcook or chicken will be tough.
5. Remove chicken with tongs and set aside on plate.
6. Add mushrooms to the pan and cook for 5 minutes.
7. Add wine and reduce for 2 minutes while scraping up bits of chicken with a wooden spoon.
8. Add chicken stock and cook for 5 minutes.
9. Add parsley and remaining 2 tablespoons butter. Cook for a minute.
10. Return chicken to pan and coat with sauce.
11. Add salt and pepper to taste.
12. Serve with rice or pasta.

THE LOVE OF CHICKEN

Another chicken recipe? Trust me, this one is guaranteed to help you impress your sweetie.

INGREDIENTS

One 3-pound chicken cut into 8 pieces or 2 smaller chickens cut into eighths (Your butcher can do this for you.)

1 1/2 cups flour seasoned with 1 tablespoon salt, 3/4 teaspoon pepper, and 3 tablespoons paprika

1 stick of unsalted butter

1 large yellow onion, peeled and chopped

2 tablespoons honey

1 teaspoon ground thyme

1 tablespoon dried thyme

3 tablespoons olive oil

1/2 teaspoon pepper

1/4 cup lemon juice

1/4 cup white wine

Salt and pepper

DIRECTIONS

1. Preheat oven to 350°F.
2. Place butter in a 12 inch x 10" inch casserole pan and heat in oven. Remove pan when butter is melted.
3. Coat chicken by tossing in bag with flour mixture.
4. Remove chicken from bag and place in pan, skin side down, with melted butter. Toss to coat.
5. Add salt and pepper to taste then bake for 30 minutes.
6. While the chicken bakes, mix the remaining ingredients in a bowl.
7. After 30 minutes, add the onion mixture to the chicken. Combine well and cover. Cook for 30 additional minutes.
8. Uncover and bake 10 more minutes until browned. Remove from oven.
9. Serve with my Baked Potato Chips or rice (see page 243). The juices from the chicken are too good to leave on the plate.

Servings: 4

Prep Time: 20 minutes

Cook Time: 1 hour

SHOPPING LIST

Need

☐ Chicken

☐ Butter

☐ Onion

May Have on Hand

☐ Honey

☐ Lemon juice

☐ Olive oil

☐ Flour

☐ Paprika

☐ Thyme (ground and dried)

☐ Salt and pepper

☐ White wine

BAKED POTATO CHIPS
Page 167

PAILLARD CHICKEN

Paillard is an older French culinary term referring to thinly sliced or pounded piece of meat that is cooked quickly. This chicken recipe is so simple, yet we all know that sometimes less can be more.

INGREDIENTS

2 butterflied chicken breasts, thinly pounded
(Your butcher can do this for you.)

2 tablespoons butter

1 tablespoon olive oil

1 lemon, quartered

Salt and pepper

DIRECTIONS

1 Season chicken with salt and pepper.

2 In a small sauté pan, heat oil and butter over low heat.

3 Preheat broiler.

4 On a large baking sheet line with non-stick foil, place the chicken and brush half of the oil or butter mixture on top. Place in broiler for two minutes per side.

5 Drizzle cooking juices over chicken. Squeeze 1 lemon wedge over each breast and serve with rice or roasted potatoes.

CAVIAR AND CREPES

There is no other specialty dish that will impress your guests like caviar. Beluga, Sevruga or Osetra are high-quality, expensive types of caviar, but there are also some wonderful less expensive American caviars readily available. Enjoy experimenting with their flavors and you'll be a caviar aficionado in no time. Crepes are the perfect accompaniment to this delicacy and are easier to make than you may think.

INGREDIENTS

3 ounces of caviar
2 hard-boiled eggs
1 small red onion, finely chopped
1 cup crème fraiche or sour cream

Crepes
1 cup flour
1/2 cup milk
Pinch salt
4 eggs, slightly beaten
1 stick unsalted butter

DIRECTIONS

1. In a medium bowl, mix flour, milk, salt, and eggs. Let rest for 20 minutes so that bubbles do not form.

2. Preheat a small nonstick fry pan over medium low heat.

3. Line a plate with a large sheet of foil. Place a large sheet of plastic wrap on top of the foil.

4. Melt butter. Dip pastry brush in melted butter, brush on the bottom of the pan and then pour 1-2 tablespoons of batter into the pan.

5. Swirl batter to cover bottom of pan and cook for 2 minutes each side. As crepes are done, place them on the plate. Repeat until all the batter is used.

6. Cover the crepes until you are ready to serve. You can also freeze them in the plastic wrap and place them in a microwave for a few seconds to heat and serve.

7. On a large service tray, arrange onions, egg whites, egg yolks, crème fraiche, and caviar.

8. Serve with the warm homemade crepes.

9. Spoon a small amount of caviar onto your crepe, add desired toppings, roll or fold, and enjoy.

Servings: **2**

Prep Time: **10 minutes**

Cook Time: **20 minutes**

SHOPPING LIST

Need
☐ Caviar
☐ Crème fraiche
☐ Eggs
☐ Red onion

May Have on Hand
☐ Butter
☐ Flour
☐ Milk
☐ Salt

TIPS

A caviar spoon is usually made from a non-metallic material such as glass or mother-of-pearl. Some food experts suggest that sterling silver transfers an unpleasant flavor to the caviar, but an inert metal such as gold will not.

Caviar can be served straight from the container. It is important that it stays cold.

If any caviar is left over, you can serve it on a baked potato or toss in pasta the next day.

A great variety of caviar is available online.

GLAZED COD
Page 101

MEATBALLS AND POTATOES
Page 105

CHICKEN ESPANOLA
Page 111

ORIENTAL CHICKEN
Page 107

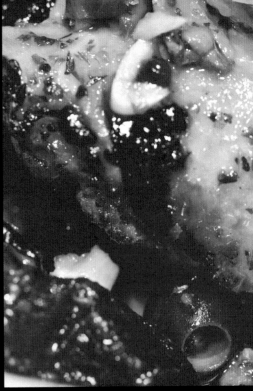

KITCHEN SINK CHICKEN Page 113

CHAPTER 4
B.Y.O.B: BRING YOUR OWN BOTTLE

It's official. You've made it to the chapter with the most TASTOSTERONE in the entire cookbook! The simple twist of a bottle cap is my quick solution for preparing stress-free meals. No need to share your little secret to culinary success.

This chapter works great for the busy weeknight dinner, but keep in mind my "Meatballs and Potatoes" are also a Sunday family favorite. A meal dressed its best with fresh ingredients or the sweet stuff from a bottle will dazzle your guests equally. Shake, then pour, and guests will be knocking down the door!

Come on, no more excuses for steering clear of the kitchen. These recipes are by far the simplest to make and enjoy. By cooking with sauces and dressings, you will become a confident chef in no time.

SOY SAUCE
+ SAKE
= GLAZED COD

Sake is a wonderful addition to fish, opening up a whole new world of tastes. Make sure to only use sake that you would drink in your cooking as it does make a difference in the flavor.

INGREDIENTS

1 tablespoon vegetable oil

3 tablespoons low sodium soy sauce

3 tablespoons sake

3 tablespoons honey

2 tablespoons dark miso paste

4 black cod fillets

1 tablespoon sesame seeds (optional)

DIRECTIONS

1 In a sauté pan large enough to hold the fish, combine all ingredients except fish and simmer for 5 minutes then cool down.

2 Place fish into the pan, coat both sides in the sauce then cover and marinate in refrigerator for 4 hours.

3 Remove from refrigerator. Over medium high heat, sear the fish for 4 minutes per side or broil for 5 - 8 minutes.

4 Serve with Japanese-style white rice and garnish with sesame seeds (optional).

Servings: **4**

Prep Time: **10 minutes**

Cook Time: **10 minutes**

SHOPPING LIST

Need

☐ Black cod

☐ Sake

May Have on Hand

☐ Vegetable oil

☐ Soy sauce

☐ Honey

☐ Miso paste

Optional

☐ Sesame seeds

SWEET AND SOUR SAUCE + TERIYAKI SAUCE = GLAZED SALMON

The sweet-salty mix of flavor in my glazed salmon meets in the middle so everyone is happy.

Pull this fish out of water when a fight is brewing in the house and you'll turn the mood around.

INGREDIENTS

One 16-ounce fresh salmon filet center cut

1 small bottle sweet and sour sauce (I prefer La Choy)

1 small bottle teriyaki sauce

DIRECTIONS

1 Preheat oven to 375°F. Place salmon on a baking sheet lined with foil.

2 Combine equal parts sweet and sour sauce and teriyaki sauce. Coat fish completely with mixture.

3 Place baking sheet with fish in the oven and bake for 20 minutes.

4 Remove from oven, add additional sweet and sour and teriyaki sauce, and bake for an additional 10 minutes.

5 Remove fish from the oven and serve with rice.

Servings: **4**

Prep Time: **5 minutes**

Cook Time: **30 minutes**

SHOPPING LIST

Need

☐ Salmon

☐ Sweet and sour sauce

☐ Teriyaki sauce

10 FL OZ (296 mL)

CHILI SAUCE
= MEATBALLS AND POTATOES

With some slaw on the side, these meatballs and potatoes are a crowd pleaser. If my retired dad can whip this up with confidence, so can you.

INGREDIENTS

1 1/2-pound ground beef or any ground meat
1 small onion, grated
1 onion, diced
1 egg
1/2 teaspoon salt
1/2 teaspoon pepper
1 piece of bread
2 tablespoons milk
1 bottle chili sauce (I prefer Heinz)
3-4 potatoes sliced into 2 inch quarters

DIRECTIONS

1 Preheat oven to 325°F.

2 Place milk in a bowl. Soak both sides of bread in milk. Squeeze bread as you would ring out a sponge.

3 In another bowl, combine meat, egg that has been whipped with a fork, grated onion, salt, pepper, and bread. Shape mixture into meatballs about 2 inches in diameter.

4 In a large casserole pot, mix diced onions, chili sauce and ketchup.

5 Place meatballs in pot on top of diced onion and chili sauce, then place potatoes over meatballs. Don't mix; leave in layers.

6 Cover pot and bake for 2 hours. Do not stir during the first hour of cooking or meatballs will fall apart. After one hour, gently toss sauce, potatoes and meatballs.

7 Remove from the oven and serve.

Servings: **8**

Prep Time: **15 minutes**

Cook Time: **2 hours**

SHOPPING LIST

Need

☐ Ground beef

☐ Potatoes

☐ Chili sauce

May Have on Hand

☐ Onions

☐ Egg

☐ Salt

☐ Pepper

☐ Bread

☐ Milk

TERIYAKI SAUCE
+ SOY SAUCE
= ORIENTAL CHICKEN

Everyone loves going out for hibachi. Now you can enjoy making your very own teriyaki. No acrobatics with knives needed!

INGREDIENTS

6 chicken thighs with bone on

6 chicken drums

6 chicken wings

1/2 cup teriyaki sauce

1/2 cup soy sauce

3 tablespoons garlic powder

DIRECTIONS

1. Season chicken with garlic powder.
2. Place the rest of the ingredients in a 1-gallon Ziploc bag then add the chicken.
3. Marinate for a minimum of 4 hours or a maximum of 24 hours.
4. Preheat oven to 350°F. Remove chicken from refrigerator and place in large baking dish. Bake chicken until golden brown, 15 - 20 minutes per side.
5. Remove chicken from the oven.
6. Preheat broiler.
7. Broil chicken for an additional 5 minutes per side.
8. Remove from broiler and serve with rice, potatoes or pasta.

Servings: **4**

Prep Time: **10 minutes**

Cook Time: **50 minutes**

SHOPPING LIST

Need

☐ Chicken

☐ Teriyaki sauce

☐ Soy sauce

May Have on Hand

☐ Garlic powder

107

CHILI SAUCE = CHICKEN AND RICE

This dish is so, so easy. It's really quick chicken cacciatore for the man who loves his chili sauce.

Don't forget to add a jar of pitted green olives to complete the dish because after all a B.Y.O.B. is all about the bottle.

INGREDIENTS

One 3-pound chicken, cut into pieces with skin removed

1 large onion, chopped

1 bottle of chili sauce (I prefer Heinz)

1 pinch pickling spice

2 tablespoons garlic powder

1 large green pepper, chopped (discard seeds and stem)

2 cups cooked white rice (see page 243 for how to cook rice)

1 can pitted green olives (optional)

DIRECTIONS

1 Preheat oven to 325°F.

2 In a large pot over medium heat combine onions, chili sauce and spices. Cook for 3 minutes.

3 Add chicken and garlic powder to the pot and toss.

4 Cover pot and cook over low flame or place in oven for 30 minutes.

5 Add pepper and rice and cook or bake for an additional 30 minutes.

6 Remove from heat and enjoy.

Servings: **4**

Prep Time: **10 minutes**

Cook Time: **40 minutes**

SHOPPING LIST

Need

☐ Chicken

☐ Onion

☐ Green pepper

☐ Chili sauce

☐ Green olives

☐ Pickling spice

May Have on Hand

☐ Garlic Powder

☐ Rice

TIP

If you have some leftover rice, this recipe is a perfect way to use it up.

SALSA
= CHICKEN ESPANOLA

I've given this recipe out so many times I can no longer count. Everyone loves it because you look like a culinary star with only the twist of a salsa jar.

Skip the hour or so of chopping up vegetables and still impress the guests, family or friends with this easy dish.

INGREDIENTS

1 large jar of your favorite salsa
  (I prefer Green Mountain Gringo salsa)

1 tablespoon garlic powder (optional)

1/2 teaspoon salt

1/2 teaspoon pepper

4 skinless chicken breasts with bone in

DIRECTIONS

1 Preheat oven to 350°F.

2 Place chicken in a large baking dish.

3 In the same baking dish, season chicken with salt, pepper and garlic powder (optional).

4 Pour jar of salsa over chicken. Make sure chicken is covered.

5 Cover with foil and bake for 40 minutes to 1 hour.

6 Serve with sides such as tortilla chips, sour cream, corn on the cob, or rice.

Servings: **4**

Prep Time: **5 minutes**

Cook Time: **45 minutes**

SHOPPING LIST

Need

☐ Chicken

☐ Salsa

May Have on Hand

☐ Salt

☐ Pepper

Optional

☐ Garlic powder

RED WINE + BLACK OLIVES + OLIVE OIL + CAPERS + WHITE WINE = KITCHEN SINK CHICKEN

This dish does not require much work to serve a large crowd. Its combination of flavors may lead guests to believe you slaved in the kitchen for hours.

Accept the kudos, but don't expect an invitation to dinner because no one will want to compete with this winning chicken dish. It's that good!

INGREDIENTS

4 chickens, cut each into 12 pieces (ask your butcher to do this for you)
1/2 teaspoon salt
1/2 teaspoon pepper
10 garlic cloves, peeled and mashed
1/2 cup dry oregano
1/2 cup red wine vinegar
One 15-ounce can or jar black olives, pitted and drained
One 15-ounce can or jar green olives, pitted and drained
1/2 cup olive oil
1 large package pitted prunes
1 small bottle green capers, drained
6 bay leaves
1/2 cup brown sugar
1 cup white wine
1 cup yellow raisins
2 tablespoons parsley, chopped (optional)
Hot sauce (optional)

DIRECTIONS

1. In a large plastic container with a lid, combine all ingredients except the chicken and optional ingredients of parsley and hot sauce.

2. Clean and dry chicken. Add chicken to the container, cover and shake so mixture covers the chicken.

3. Place in refrigerator for one day. Shake from time to time.

4. Preheat oven to 350°F.

5. Remove the container from the refrigerator and pour into two large casserole pans. Cover with foil. Bake for 1 1/2 hours until chicken is cooked through. Remove from oven.

6. If you prefer your chicken well done like I do, remove foil and broil for 5 minutes or until golden brown.

Servings: **12**

Prep Time: **10 minutes**

Cook Time: **90 minutes**

SHOPPING LIST

Need
- ☐ Chicken
- ☐ Garlic cloves
- ☐ Black olives
- ☐ Prunes
- ☐ Green olives
- ☐ Capers
- ☐ Yellow raisins

May Have on Hand
- ☐ Oregano
- ☐ Red wine vinegar
- ☐ Olive oil
- ☐ Bay leaves
- ☐ Brown sugar
- ☐ White wine
- ☐ Salt and pepper

Optional
- ☐ Parsley
- ☐ Hot sauce

TIP

Serve this dish with couscous, which can be made ahead of time.

FRENCH DRESSING
+ DUCK SAUCE
= ORANGE CHICKEN

This is a true B.Y.O.B. recipe. It's sweet, tart and savory thanks to just a few bottles.

It's full of TASTOSTERONE and impossible to screw up!

INGREDIENTS

Two 3-pound chickens, cut into 8 pieces

1 bottle country-style French salad dressing

1 bottle duck sauce
(I prefer Saucy Susan Duck Sauce)

1 packet onion soup mix
(I prefer Lipton's Onion Soup Mix)

DIRECTIONS

1 Preheat oven to 350°F.

2 In a tin baking pan, combine French dressing, duck sauce and onion soup mix. (I use a disposable pan so you can discard the super sticky container when done cooking.)

3 Add chicken to mixture and toss. Cover with foil and bake for 1 hour.

4 For crispier chicken, broil for an additional 4 minutes (optional).

5 Serve with rice or roasted potatoes.

Servings: **6**

Prep Time: **5 minutes**

Cook Time: **1 hour**

SHOPPING LIST

Need

☐ Chicken

☐ French dressing

☐ Duck sauce

☐ Onion soup mix

LEMON JUICE + WHITE WINE + CHICKEN BROTH = LEMON CHICKEN

My girlfriend Wendy and her husband Greg, a true TASTOSTERONE couple, cook her mom's Lemon Chicken recipe quite often. They recommend serving this dish with rice or potatoes and enjoy every drop of this delicious sauce.

INGREDIENTS

2/3 cup lemon juice
1/2 cup white wine
One 15-ounce can condensed chicken broth
1 egg
Four 4-ounce boneless, skinless chicken breasts, thinly pounded
1 cup seasoned breadcrumbs
   (Wendy & Greg prefer JASON Flavored Breadcrumbs)
3 tablespoons vegetable oil
Fresh parsley, chopped (optional)
Salt and pepper

DIRECTIONS

1 In small sauté pan simmer lemon juice, wine and soup for 5 minutes. Set aside.

2 Season chicken with salt and pepper.

3 Crack egg in bowl and whisk. Place breadcrumbs in another bowl.

4 Dip seasoned chicken in egg, then breadcrumbs.

5 Heat oil in sauté pan.

6 Sauté chicken in oil 2 minutes per side or until golden brown.

7 Place chicken on a serving plate and pour lemon sauce on top.

8 Garnish with parsley (optional).

Servings: 4

Prep Time: **15 minutes**

Cook Time: **20 minutes**

SHOPPING LIST

Need

☐ Chicken

☐ Chicken broth

May Have on Hand

☐ Lemon juice

☐ White wine

☐ Egg

☐ Breadcrumbs

☐ Vegetable oil

Optional

☐ Parsley

ROTISSERIE CHICKEN SALAD
Page 129

PANINI SANDWICHES
Page 131

CHAPTER 5
BAG IT: LUNCH

Leftovers get a bad "wrap" and now the time has come to sack their sad reputation for not satisfying a hungry man. Recycling a meal not only saves time and money, it's also another reminder that cooking can be creative and recipes need not apply. Pass on the fast food and consider bagging "My Mother's Meatloaf" leftovers from the previous night's dinner. Just thinly slice the meat, add a touch of mayo and enjoy your new creation on toast or tasty ciabatta bread. Lunch does not get better than this mouthwatering meatloaf sandwich!

You could also showcase your culinary skills with a large pot of "Swiss Mac and Cheese." This homemade favorite tastes miles better than a box packed with preservatives. The kids will thank you for it.

I also highly recommend owning a panini maker. They're fun to use and can quickly make dozens of different lunch combinations. So try some of my effortless lunch recipes and sandwich suggestions, bag it and flex your TASTOSTERONE.

CROQUE MONSIEUR

Oo-la-la... even if you can't speak a word of French this sandwich will speak for you. Impress your friends with a tasty Croque Monsieur. Okay, so it's just a fancy name for a ham and cheese sandwich, but nothing beats its simple goodness. Thanks to the wide selection of panini makers currently on the market, cooking this classic is now a breeze. You can even create your own sandwich combinations in seconds. No mess, no fuss.

INGREDIENTS

2 slices of your favorite bread

1/2 tablespoon mayonnaise

1 teaspoon Dijon mustard

2 slices deli ham

2 slices Gruyère cheese

1 tablespoon unsalted butter, softened

DIRECTIONS

1. Preheat panini maker or large non-stick pan.
2. Spread mayonnaise on one side of a slice of bread and mustard on the other.
3. Top the mayonnaise side with one slice of ham, then cheese, followed by ham and cheese again.
4. Fold to make a sandwich and butter the outside of the bread.
5. Cut off crust.
6. Press in panini maker and cook until the cheese melts and the bread is golden brown. If using a non-stick pan, press bread down with a second pan. Turn over with a spatula and toast the other side.
7. Cut in half and serve.

Servings: **1**

Prep Time: **5 minutes**

Cook Time: **5 minutes**

SHOPPING LIST

Need

☐ Ham

☐ Gruyère cheese

May Have on Hand

☐ Bread

☐ Butter

☐ Mayonnaise

☐ Dijon mustard

TIPS

Experiment with different breads when making this classic sandwich. There are many varieties of healthy, hearty breads available at your local supermarket.

This dish is also delicious served with small Cornichon-style pickles.

SWISS MAC AND CHEESE

Once you try a Swiss-influenced macaroni and cheese recipe, there will be no turning back. Young or old, everyone craves this cheesy comfort food.

INGREDIENTS

6 cups milk, whole or low fat
1 teaspoon salt
1 package of elbow macaroni or any other type of pasta
1 1/2 cups Gruyère cheese, grated
2 teaspoons pepper
1 1/2 sticks unsalted butter
2 small onions, sliced
1 shallot, sliced
1 garlic clove, chopped

DIRECTIONS

1 Heat milk and salt in a large pot over high heat until boiling.

2 Add macaroni or pasta, reduce heat and simmer uncovered. Cook for 20 minutes, stirring occasionally. Pasta should soften. Add additional milk if needed.

3 Preheat oven to 350°F and place an empty casserole dish or ovenproof pot in the oven.

4 Pour pasta (do not drain) into preheated pot. Add cheese and pepper to the mixture and stir.

5 Cover and bake for 10 minutes.

6 While pasta is baking, melt butter over medium heat in medium sauté pan. Add onions and garlic. Heat until very crispy. Top the pasta and cheese with the sautéed onion mixture.

7 Bake in 400°F oven for 5 minutes or until pasta is brown.

8 Remove from oven and serve.

Servings: **4**

Prep Time: **20 minutes**

Cook Time:
35 - 40 minutes

SHOPPING LIST

Need

☐ Pasta

☐ Gruyère cheese

☐ Cream cheese

☐ Onions

☐ Shallot

☐ Garlic

May Have on Hand

☐ Milk

☐ Butter

☐ Salt

☐ Pepper

CHICKEN PITA

Everyone loves a rotisserie chicken from the local deli or supermarket. Why not use the chicken meat to also make a light, simple lunch or snack?

INGREDIENTS

1/2 cup rotisserie chicken off the bone, skin removed and shredded

1/4 cup iceberg lettuce, shredded

1 squeeze of fresh lemon

1 tablespoon Parmesan cheese, grated

Pita bread, toasted

Salt and pepper

DIRECTIONS

1 Mix together all ingredients, except pita bread.

2 Stuff chicken salad into a lightly toasted pita or serve in a bowl with bread or crackers on the side.

Servings: 1

Prep Time: **5 minutes**

Cook Time: **None**

SHOPPING LIST

Need

☐ Chicken

☐ Iceberg lettuce

☐ Pita bread

May Have on Hand

☐ Lemon

☐ Parmesan cheese

☐ Salt and pepper

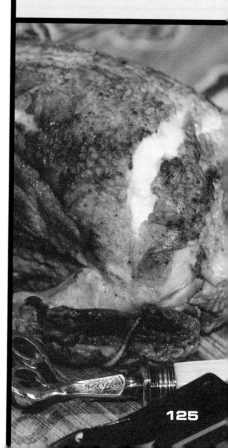

125

SHRIMP AND AVOCADO

When I was a senior at Syracuse University, I studied abroad in London for a year. Like any college student I had a limited budget, but a bug to travel. One way I saved was to eat this protein-packed meal every day for weeks. You would think seafood would be expensive, but it really wasn't because I bought everything at the local farmer's market. I enjoyed this meal so much that I rarely had the craving to waste money on eating out. Thanks to this dish, I enjoyed traveling across the United Kingdom, Italy and Switzerland.

Now, that's something to chew on.

INGREDIENTS

2 ripe avocados (I prefer the Haas brand)

1/2 cup frozen or fresh pre-cooked shrimp
  (I prefer baby or small shrimp)

2 tablespoons mayonnaise

2 tablespoons ketchup

DIRECTIONS

1 Slice avocado in half. Remove pit and skin.

2 Combine mayonnaise and ketchup. (You've just made Russian dressing!)

3 Plate the avocados, top with shrimp then spoon dressing over shrimp. Add salt and pepper to taste.

4 Enjoy and happy travels!

TIP

I sometimes just leave the avocado in the shell, stuff the shrimp in the center of the avocados, and then drizzle the dressing on top.

It saves on preparation time and is attractive to serve.

Servings: **2**

Prep Time: **5 minutes**

Cook Time: **None**

SHOPPING LIST

Need

☐ Avocados

☐ Shrimp

May Have on Hand

☐ Mayonnaise

☐ Ketchup

HOW TO REMOVE AN AVOCADO PIT Page 253

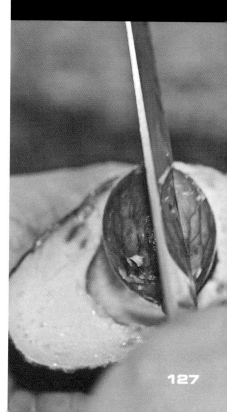

ROTISSERIE CHICKEN SALAD

My girlfriend's husband, the main cook in her household for 30 plus years (an original T-Man), shared this recipe with me. If you have some leftover pasta and a rotisserie chicken, no cooking is necessary. It's basically assembly. If you can change a tire, you can make this recipe.

INGREDIENTS

1/4 cup soy sauce

1/4 cup peanut butter

1/4 cup rice wine vinegar

2 tablespoons sugar

1 tablespoon Tahini (you can find this in the international section of your grocer)

2 teaspoons sweet chili sauce

1 package frozen snow pea pods or sugar snap peas, thawed and drained

1 package pasta, cooked

1 rotisserie chicken, remove skin and bones, shred meat (many supermarkets have cooked rotisserie chickens readily available)

2 tablespoons sesame seeds

2 scallions or spring onions, cut into 1-inch pieces

DIRECTIONS

1 In a large glass bowl, combine soy sauce, peanut butter, vinegar, sugar, tahini and chili sauce.

2 Add thawed snow peas, cooked pasta and chicken. Mix well.

3 In same bowl, top with sesame seeds and chopped scallion/ spring onions.

4 Serve chilled, warm, or at room temperature.

Servings: **6**

Prep Time: **10 minutes**

Cook Time: **10 minutes**

SHOPPING LIST

Need
- [ ] Chicken
- [ ] Peas
- [ ] Scallions or onions
- [ ] Tahini
- [ ] Pasta

May Have on Hand
- [ ] Soy sauce
- [ ] White vinegar
- [ ] Chili sauce
- [ ] Peanut butter
- [ ] Sugar
- [ ] Sesame seeds

TIPS

Try to buy a pre-cooked rotisserie chicken that has not been plumped up with salt and preservatives. Bigger is not always better.

Sesame seeds tend to spoil quickly. Keep them in the freezer for a longer shelf life.

PANINI SANDWICH COMBINATIONS

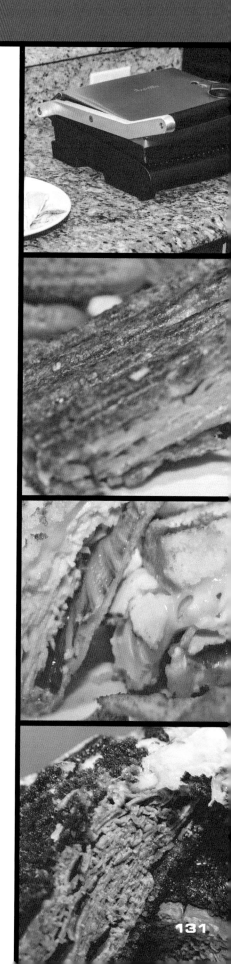

For scrumptious Panini sandwiches choose breads like wraps, multigrains, croissants, focaccia, or rye breads. Experiment with combinations of ingredients and breads to create your own signature Panini sandwiches.

ALL GOOD THINGS COME IN THREES!

- Bacon, Swiss cheese and mayo
- Grilled vegetables, greens and feta cheese
- Corned beef, Swiss cheese and Russian dressing
- Steak, roasted peppers and cheese
- Tuna, American cheese and tomato
- Brie, green apple and baked ham
- A Jersey classic – fried egg, pork roll and cheese

SOME OTHER FAVORITES

- Grilled chicken, tomato sauce, mozzarella, and Parmesan cheese
- Pulled pork, ham, Swiss cheese, pickles, and mustard
- Gruyère cheese and sliced tomatoes with cracked pepper
- Tofu, eggplant, mozzarella cheese topped with tomato sauce and basil

TIPS

Butter up! Make sure to butter the inside and outside of the bread to ensure a better grill effect. The cheese on the inside works like glue, holding the sandwich together.

Tofu can also be a replacement for any meat.

ARUGULA SALAD
Page 149

**CRT'S (CUCUMBER, RADISH AND
CHERRY TOMATO SALAD** Page 139

**ALL YOU CAN EAT
SALAD** Page 147

**BLUE CHEESE
DRESSING** Page 157

**MOZZARELLA
SALAD** Page 143

When I was a young girl I loved the joke, "Do you have olive oil in a can? Yes! Well you better let her out because Popeye is mad." Like Popeye, I'm mad about olive oil and my spinach. In this chapter, I share some easy tips for enjoying your leafy greens and other veggies.

My "Soft Taco Veggie Stir-fry" is packed with nutritious vegetables all wrapped up in a taco shell. Big muscles are not required for these recipes, but you must eat your veggies to make sure you're getting those super important vitamins and minerals.

Thanks to my simply delicious recipes and a little help from olive oil, you'll enjoy your vegetables without having to open a can like Popeye.

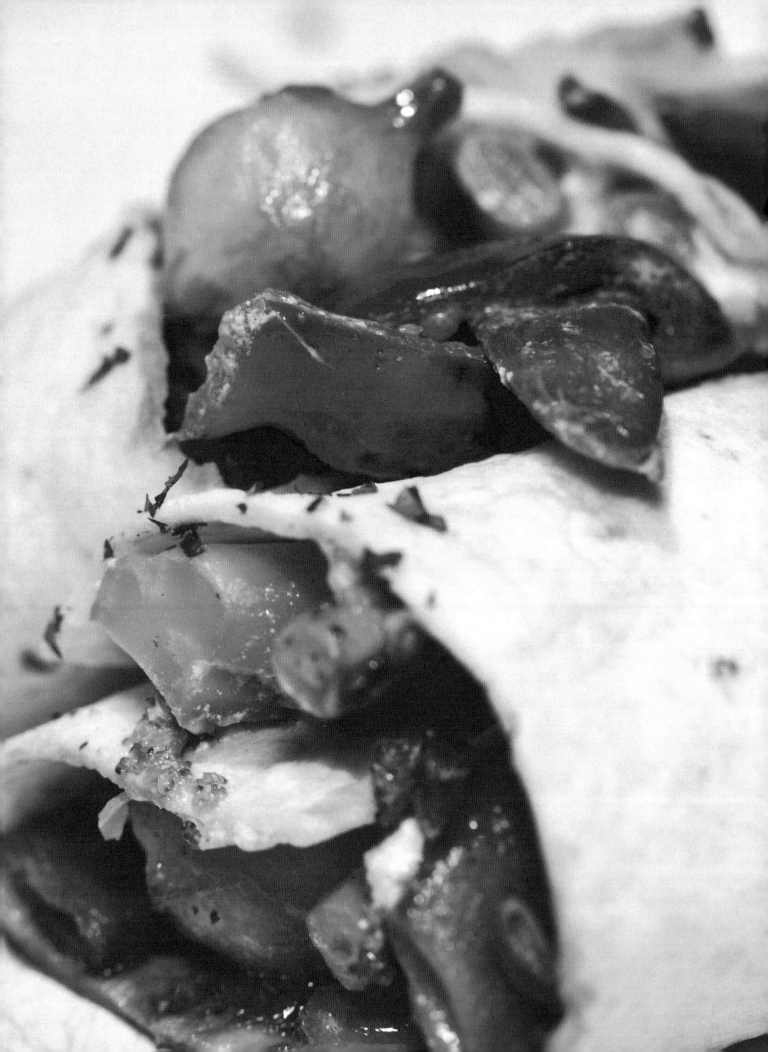

SOFT TACO VEGETABLE STIR-FRY

I've been making this dish for years. I started cooking it at Syracuse University when my roommates and I were starving and craving a simple veggie dish. I also cooked up this recipe when my daughter was very little to introduce her to vegetables. Now she is fan of almost all vegetables. T-Men, this is a healthy way to eat your greens. Feel free to use the vegetables listed below or whatever you have on hand.

INGREDIENTS

2 tablespoons vegetable oil
2 carrots, cut into 1-inch long slices
1 onion, coarsely chopped
1 head of broccoli, cut into small pieces
1 zucchini or yellow squash, sliced into half moons
1 1/2 cups snow pea pods or sugar snap peas, fresh or frozen (thawed)
1/4 cup sour cream
3 tablespoons soy sauce
1/2 teaspoon salt
1/2 teaspoon pepper
1/4 cup Parmesan cheese, freshly grated
4 soft tortillas, warmed in toaster or oven
Hot sauce (optional)

DIRECTIONS

1 In a wok or very large sauté pan, add oil and heat over medium heat.

2 Add carrots, onions, and broccoli to wok/pan and cook for 5-8 minutes over medium heat or to desired crispness.

3 Add the remaining vegetables and toss with tongs or a wooden spoon. Remove from heat when vegetables are tender, about 3 minutes.

4 Add soy sauce, sour cream, salt, and pepper to sautéed vegetables and toss to coat.

5 Spoon mixture into warm tortillas and fold.

6 Add a dash of hot sauce (optional) and Parmesan cheese. Enjoy.

Servings: 4

Prep Time: 10 minutes

Cook Time: 15 minutes

SHOPPING LIST

Need

☐ Broccoli
☐ Carrots
☐ Onion
☐ Snow pea pods
   or sugar snap peas
☐ Squash
☐ Parmesan cheese
☐ Sour cream
☐ Soft tortillas

May Have on Hand

☐ Soy sauce
☐ Vegetable oil
☐ Salt and pepper

Optional

☐ Hot sauce

TIPS

You can add chicken, steak or shrimp to this dish during Step 3.

Sautéed vegetables also make great toppings for baked potatoes, pasta and rice.

BEETS, NUTS & BLUE

The charming Camden Harbour Inn in Maine serves an out-of-this-world beet and blue cheese salad. This recipe is my adaptation of the dish. The high iron content of beets regenerates and reactivates the red blood cells and supplies fresh oxygen to the body, so come on guys – charge up and try these delicious beets.

Servings: 2

Prep Time: **10 minutes**

Cook Time: **None**

INGREDIENTS

1 pound package fresh cooked beets (See Tip)

1/2 cup blue cheese, sliced or crumbled

2 tablespoons extra virgin olive oil

1/4 cup candied walnuts, coarsely chopped

Salt and pepper

SHOPPING LIST

Need

☐ Beets

☐ Blue cheese

☐ Candied walnuts

May Have on Hand

☐ Olive oil

☐ Salt and pepper

DIRECTIONS

1 Cut beets into 1/4-inch slices and arrange on plate.

2 Sprinkle beets with blue cheese or layer the blue cheese between the beet slices.

3 Sprinkle nuts on top and drizzle with oil.

4 Add salt and pepper to taste.

TIPS

To save time, cooked beets can be found pre-packaged in the produce section of your supermarket.

Remember, beets stain everything... hands, counters, and cutting boards, so cut on a plate for easy cleanup. Be careful not to get the juice on your hands.

CRT's (CUCUMBER, RADISH & CHERRY TOMATO SALAD

I attended a cooking class in France where the chef prepared an apero. He poured a chilled glass of French White Bordeaux and offered us a simple bite of cucumbers, radishes, and cherry tomatoes to accompany it. It was so refreshing! A CRT Salad is a perfect treat for guests, a romantic date or even an afternoon snack for your kids.

Servings: 4

Prep Time: 5 minutes

Cook Time: None

INGREDIENTS

1 container of grape or small cherry tomatoes, halved

6 radishes, tops removed and cut into quarters

1 cucumber, peeled, seeded and cut into 1/2-inch cubes

1 tablespoon fig, balsamic or red wine vinegar

2 -3 tablespoons extra virgin olive oil

1- 2 teaspoons salt (I prefer sea salt)

1/2 teaspoon freshly ground black pepper

2 tablespoons scallions, chopped

SHOPPING LIST

Need

☐ Cucumber

☐ Radishes

☐ Tomatoes (grape or cherry)

☐ Scallions

May Have on Hand

☐ Vinegar

☐ Olive oil

☐ Salt and pepper

DIRECTIONS

1 Combine salt, pepper, vinegar and oil in the bottom of a small bowl.

2 Add all the CRTs (cucumbers, radish and cherry tomatoes) and toss.

3 Add additional salt and pepper to taste.

4 Serve in a bowl with toothpicks on the side.

SLAW

This slaw is so easy and delicious no one will believe you really made it. Guys, pass on the deli counter this time, this slaw is a winner.

INGREDIENTS

1 head of white cabbage, shredded (See Tip)

1 cucumber, thinly sliced

1 small red onion, thinly sliced

1/2 cup carrots, grated (about 2 carrots) (See Tip)

1 tablespoon sugar

1 small jar pickle relish

1/2 cup sour cream

1/2 cup mayonnaise

Salt and black pepper

DIRECTIONS

1 In a large glass bowl, mix all ingredients.

2 Cover and refrigerate for 2 hours, or until the cabbage has softened. While in the refrigerator, stir a few times to blend.

3 Remove from refrigerator and serve.

Servings: **6**

Prep Time: **10 minutes**

Cook Time: **None**

SHOPPING LIST

Need

☐ Cabbage
☐ Carrots
☐ Cucumber
☐ Red onion
☐ Relish
☐ Sour cream

May Have on Hand

☐ Sugar
☐ Mayonnaise
☐ Salt and pepper

TIPS

Many stores sell packaged pre-shredded cabbage and carrots, which save time on preparation.

You can also substitute broccoli slaw for cabbage.

CLASSIC MOZZARELLA SALAD

This recipe tastes best when you use fresh ingredients. You'll find that there is nothing like a fresh Jersey tomato on a hot August day. If you're not in New Jersey, any local farm-raised tomato will come in second.

INGREDIENTS

2 pounds tomatoes (about 5), sliced thin or thick

1 pound fresh mozzarella

1 bunch fresh basil, chopped, stems removed (roughly 10 leaves)

2 tablespoons extra virgin olive oil

2 tablespoons red wine vinegar

1 tablespoon balsamic vinegar

Salt and pepper

DIRECTIONS

1. Alternate tomato and mozzarella slices on a plate to make a tower.
2. Sprinkle chopped basil over the top.
3. Drizzle oil and vinegars over the top.
4. Add salt and pepper to taste.
5. Best served at room temperature and with a crusty piece of Italian bread.

TIP

Some specialty stores make their own mozzarella, which is well worth the trip to purchase.

Servings: **4**

Prep Time: **5 minutes**

Cook Time: **None**

SHOPPING LIST

Need

☐ Basil

☐ Mozzarella

☐ Tomatoes

May Have on Hand

☐ Olive oil

☐ Balsamic vinegar

☐ Red Wine vinegar

☐ Salt and pepper

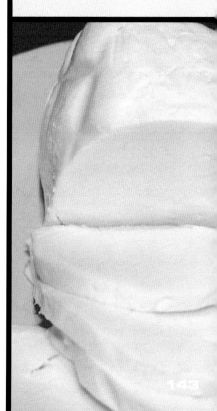

ISRAELI SALAD

Down for dicing? Distinguished by the tiny diced tomatoes and cucumbers, this salad is considered the most well-known national dish of Israel. Each ingredient is perfectly chopped for a tasteful bite.

My version is never perfect, nor does a T-Man's have to be.

This salad is a great accompaniment to my Lamb Chop Bites (see page 21).

INGREDIENTS

1 medium red onion, finely diced
1 red or green bell pepper, seeds removed and diced
3 medium tomatoes, seeds discarded and diced
1 cucumber, diced
2 celery stalks, diced
2 teaspoons extra virgin olive oil
Juice of 1 lemon or lime
2 tablespoons fresh parsley, chopped
Salt and pepper

DIRECTIONS

1 Mix all ingredients.

2 Add salt and pepper to taste.

TIP

Don't add the lemon/lime, salt and pepper (dressing) too early or the salad will get soggy. It's best to make it fresh, right before serving.

Servings: **4**

Prep Time: **10 minutes**

Cook Time: **None**

SHOPPING LIST

Need

☐ Celery

☐ Cucumber

☐ Red onion

☐ Fresh parsley

☐ Peppers

☐ Tomatoes

May Have on Hand

☐ Lemon or lime

☐ Olive oil

☐ Salt and pepper

ALL YOU CAN EAT SALAD

These are my favorite salad ingredients, but once you get into the groove of making salads you'll create your own mix of preferred veggies.

Servings: **4**

Prep Time: **5 minutes**

Cook Time: **None**

INGREDIENTS

1 1/2 tablespoons red wine or balsamic vinegar (or your favorite flavor)
3 tablespoons extra-virgin olive oil
1/2 head lettuce (any kind, torn with hands or chopped)
1/2 cucumber, sliced
1/4 small red onion, thinly sliced
2 tomatoes, diced or 1/2 pint of cherry tomatoes
1/2 5-ounce can garbanzo beans, drained
2 scallions, chopped
2 carrots, grated
Any type of cheese (I prefer goat, blue or any soft cheese)
Croutons
Salt and pepper

DIRECTIONS

1 Add salt and pepper to a large salad bowl. Add vinegar then mix with a fork.

2 Using a whisk or a fork drizzle in the olive oil.

3 Top dressing with lettuce and salad ingredients. Don't toss until you are ready to serve.

4 Add salt and pepper to taste.

5 Top with croutons and serve.

SHOPPING LIST

Need
- [ ] Carrots
- [ ] Cucumber
- [ ] Lettuce
- [ ] Onion
- [ ] Scallions
- [ ] Tomatoes
- [ ] Cheese
- [ ] Croutons

May Have on Hand
- [ ] Vinegar
- [ ] Olive oil
- [ ] Salt and pepper

ARUGULA SALAD

Top any dish with this peppery salad. It adds a new taste sensation and you will save time on cleanup because you use one dish for your salad and main course.

A true TASTOSTERONE chef knows how to work the kitchen and cleanup by using minimal plates and pots.

INGREDIENTS

2 cups fresh arugula, chopped

1/4 cup Parmesan cheese (use a carrot peeler to shave off slices of cheese)

3 tablespoons extra virgin olive oil

Salt and pepper

DIRECTIONS

1. Chop arugula and place in a bowl.

2. Top with Parmesan cheese and drizzle with oil. Toss.

3. Add salt and pepper to taste and serve.

TIPS

This salad has stand alone power and also works as a great side with some cured meats such as salami or prosciutto.

Compliment your creation with a glass of full-bodied red wine.

Servings: **4**

Prep Time: **5 minutes**

Cook Time: **None**

SHOPPING LIST

Need

☐ Arugula

☐ Parmesan cheese

May Have on Hand

☐ Olive oil

☐ Salt and pepper

BRUSCHETTA

Bruschetta is also another one of my favorite toppings that I often add to my Veal Milanese or any grilled meat or fish. It's also wonderful on some crusty sliced bread. Top grilled bread with bruschetta and drizzle on some good quality extra virgin olive oil.

INGREDIENTS

1 tablespoon extra virgin olive oil

1 cup plum tomatoes, seeds discarded and chopped

1 clove of garlic, mashed or finely chopped

10 fresh basil leaves, roughly chopped

DIRECTIONS

1 In a small bowl, combine all ingredients.

2 Add salt and pepper to taste.

3 Spoon mixture over toasted bread and drizzle with extra virgin oil to taste. May also be served as a topping on meats or fish. Enjoy.

Servings: **4**

Prep Time: **10 minutes**

Cook Time: **None**

SHOPPING LIST

Need

☐ Plum tomatoes

☐ Fresh basil

May Have on Hand

☐ Garlic

☐ Olive oil

VEAL MILANESE
Page 89

ONE SALAD AT A TIME DRESSING

This dressing is perfect for a couple, family of four, or more. Just keep doubling the ingredients to prepare the right amount for your crowd.

INGREDIENTS

1/2 teaspoon salt

1/2 teaspoon freshly ground black pepper

1 1/2 tablespoons red wine or balsamic vinegar (or your favorite flavor)

3 tablespoons extra-virgin olive oil

DIRECTIONS

1 Mix all ingredients.

2 Add salt and pepper to taste.

TIP

Before adding the lettuce and vegetables to your salad bowl, pour the desired amount of dressing into the bottom of the bowl.

By tossing it just before you are ready to serve, the lettuce will not wilt before guests have a chance to enjoy the salad and they can add more dressing if desired.

Servings: **2**

Prep Time: **5 minutes**

Cook Time: **None**

SHOPPING LIST

May Have on Hand

☐ Olive oil

☐ Vinegar

☐ Salt and pepper

EVERYDAY VINAIGRETTE

You're a cook with TASTOSTERONE now, so why not make your own dressing?

It's easy, tastes fresher, and blows away those store bought dressings. Go the extra mile by whipping up this vinaigrette.

Servings: **10**

Prep Time: **5 minutes**

Cook Time: **None**

INGREDIENTS

6 tablespoons red wine vinegar

1/4 teaspoon dry, ground or Dijon mustard

1 shallot, finely chopped

1/2 cup olive oil

1/4 cup extra virgin olive oil

Salt and pepper

SHOPPING LIST

Need

☐ Shallot
☐ Prosciutto

May Have on Hand

☐ Red wine vinegar
☐ Mustard
☐ Olive Oil
☐ Extra virgin olive oil
☐ Salt and pepper

DIRECTIONS

1. Mix ingredients (except oil) together with a fork or whisk, then whisk in the oil.

2. Store in an airtight container in a cool place. No need to refrigerate – the dressing will last up to a week.

3. Give it a quick whisk/stir prior to serving.

This is a versatile dressing. You can experiment with flavors by doing the following:

Option 1: Add a fresh herb like chopped rosemary and crushed garlic cloves.

Option 2: Change up the recipe by using various types of vinegars, such as champagne, tarragon and balsamic.

Option 3: Toss with some grated Parmesan cheese for a creamier dressing.

BLUE CHEESE DRESSING

Bring on the cheese. This recipe is super easy to make and well worth the minimal effort.

Guys, remember to save some dressing for your "Wing It" appetizer.

Servings: 8-12

Prep Time: **5 minutes**

Cook Time: **None**

INGREDIENTS

1 container blue cheese dressing (Blue cheese dressing can be found in the refrigerated section of the grocery store. The fewer preservatives the better the taste.)

2 ounces fresh blue cheese, crumbled (I prefer Maytag blue cheese)

DIRECTIONS

1 Mix together fresh blue cheese and dressing.

2 Chill and serve over lettuce and a few tomato slices or with chicken wings.

SHOPPING LIST

Need

☐ Blue cheese

☐ Blue cheese dressing

WING IT
Page 27

RUSSIAN DRESSING

Everyone loves the sweet taste of Russian dressing. Try it on veggie burgers, raw carrots, and don't forget that Reuben sandwich.

It's now up to you, as a seasoned TASTOSTERONE chef, to come up with your own combinations for this "can do no wrong" dressing.

INGREDIENTS

2 tablespoons ketchup

2 tablespoons mayonnaise

DIRECTIONS

1 Mix ketchup and mayonnaise in a small bowl.

2 Serve.

TIP

Add a shake of cayenne pepper or some pickle relish for a twist on this traditional Russian Dressing (sometimes referred to as Thousand Island.)

Servings: **2**

Prep Time: **1 minute**

Cook Time: **None**

SHOPPING LIST

May Have on Hand

☐ Ketchup

☐ Mayonnaise

STUFFED ARTICHOKES

For the novice T-Man, this stuffed artichoke recipe can be little daunting. Try to remember, with a little help from TASTOSTERONE and a desire to cook, everything works out in the kitchen and nothing needs to be exact. These artichokes are one of my favorites, and the saltiness of the Italian salami adds a unique twist to this classic.

INGREDIENTS

2 lemons

6 medium to large artichokes

2 cups breadcrumbs

1/4 cup flat leaf parsley, chopped

2 garlic cloves, mashed

1/2 cup mozzarella cheese, coarsely shredded

1/4 cup Italian salami, chopped into small pieces

DIRECTIONS

1. Preheat oven to 325°F.

2. Using a serrated knife cut 1 1/2 inches off the top of the artichoke. Discard the top. Cut off the bottom stem, creating a flat bottom.

3. Carefully snip off the triangular tips of the remaining leaves with scissors. Once all the leaves are trimmed, separate them to make room for the stuffing.

4. Squeeze the juice of two lemons into a large bowl of roughly 2 - 3 quarts of cold water.

5. Place in the bowl with lemon and water until ready to cook. This will prevent the artichokes from browning.

6. Mix all ingredients together in a bowl except the oil and artichokes.

7. Add olive oil a little at a time to mixture until moist, but not too wet.

8. Remove artichokes from bowl. Shake off excess water and stuff breadcrumb mixture between each leaf.

9. Place stuffed artichokes in an ovenproof baking dish.

10. Add hot water to the baking dish. Water should barely touch the bottom leaves of the artichoke. Squeeze 1/2 of a lemon into the water.

11. Cover and bake for 45 minutes or until leaves loosen. Artichokes are done when a leaf can be pulled off easily.

12. Remove from the oven and serve warm with a wedge of lemon and chopped parsley for garnish.

RECYCLED FRIED RICE
Page 175

SWISS ROSTI STYLE POTATO PANCAKES
Page 165

BAKED POTATO CHIPS Page 167

MUSHROOMS ON TOAST

PESTO PASTA

CHAPTER 7

DO YOU REALLY NEED SOMETHING ON THE SIDE?

For those of you who enjoyed the 1989 movie classic "When Harry Met Sally," you'll remember how Sally wanted everything on the side or nothing at all.

I dare my TASTOSTERONE chef to give every extraordinary side in this chapter the starring role on his plate and nothing less. A recipe like "Go for the Green" beautifully dresses breads, steak, chicken, and fish. Garlic Bread may not work for a first date, but the seasoned couple should not pass it up. Guests will appreciate a man for whatever wonderful dinner combinations he comes up with because at this point in his cooking career, he has become a confident TASTOSTERONE chef.

SWISS ROSTI STYLE POTATO PANCAKES

I fell head over heels for this dish from the moment I first had it. The first time I enjoyed Rosti (pronounced Rooschti) was at a dinner party in Switzerland. This traditional Swiss potato pancake was served with Veal in Cream Sauce. (See page 47 for recipe.) The taste of the creamy sauce from the sautéed veal was the perfect compliment to the buttery potatoes. Rosti is served many different ways and you'll enjoy every one! Toss in some chopped onions, diced ham, shredded cheese, and follow Step 2. Crack open an egg on top and bake in oven for 5 minutes for a traditional mountain meal. This dish can be served as the main event or on the side.

INGREDIENTS

2 pounds or 4 large Idaho potatoes, peeled and shredded
4 tablespoons unsalted butter
1 teaspoon kosher salt

DIRECTIONS

1. Peel the potatoes, then grate by hand with a grater or food processor.
2. Remove any excess water (see tips) before cooking the potatoes if you using a food processor. In a large non-stick frying pan, over medium heat, melt the butter.
3. Add the grated potatoes to the pan, season with salt then toss potatoes until coated with butter. Cook for 3 minutes.
4. Using a large wooden spoon or spatula press the potatoes down into the pan using the back of the spoon/spatula to form one large pancake.
5. Cover and cook for 20 minutes until sides of potatoes start to brown.
6. Carefully remove the large potato pancake from the pan and place on a plate.
7. Flip the potatoes onto another plate then slip potatoes back onto pan and continue to cook potatoes on other side.
8. Cover and cook for 15-20 additional minutes or until potatoes are golden brown.
9. Plate, cut into wedges or serve whole (if serving as a single dinner serve whole and now top with the fried egg) and enjoy.

Servings: **6**

Prep Time: **10 minutes**

Cook Time:
30-40 minutes

SHOPPING LIST

Need

☐ Potatoes

May Have on Hand

☐ Butter

☐ Salt

TIPS

For cooking, your potato needs to be firm with a dark russet-brown color on the outside, denoting it's a starchy potato.

Par boil potato to expedite cooking time.

Use paper towels to dry out any excess water from these starchy spuds.

There are many types of food processors on the market, but for this recipe you will need the best one for grating. I prefer my Cuisinart, however any one will work. The most important thing is to use the grating blade when preparing the potatoes.

BAKED POTATO CHIPS

I started making baked potato chips years ago because I love French fries.

This recipe was a way for me to enjoy my potatoes without the mess of a fryer. It's also a much healthier choice that doesn't sacrifice the flavor. T-Men, skip the fast food drive-thru and try these!

INGREDIENTS

4 Idaho potatoes skin on and thinly sliced (about 1/8 - 1/4 inch thick)

3 tablespoons olive oil

Sea salt and fresh ground pepper to taste

DIRECTIONS

1. Preheat oven to 425°F.
2. Scrub and slice potatoes, then dry with paper towels.
3. Place sliced potatoes in a large plastic bag. Add oil to the bag and shake to combine.
4. Line a baking sheet with non-stick foil. Remove potatoes from the bag and spread evenly onto foil.
5. Season with salt and pepper.
6. Bake 20 - 30 minutes or until desired crispness. (Watch them carefully so they do not burn.)
7. Remove potatoes from the oven and season again with a little salt and pepper to taste. (I sometimes sprinkle Parmesan cheese on top.)
8. Serve while hot and enjoy.

Servings: **4**

Prep Time: **15 minutes**

Cook Time: **30 minutes**

SHOPPING LIST

Need

☐ Potatoes

May Have on Hand

☐ Olive oil

☐ Salt and pepper

MUSHROOMS ON TOAST

Mushrooms on toast make a great light dinner or even a topping on grilled steaks. It's so simple, creamy and packed with flavor that you'll want to eat it straight from the pot.

Servings: **4**

Prep Time: **5 minutes**

Cook Time: **15 minutes**

INGREDIENTS

1 pound fresh white mushrooms, cleaned, stems trimmed and sliced (wipe mushrooms with a paper towel to clean)

One 15-ounce can cream of mushroom soup (Grandma used Campbell's... Mmm, Mmm good!)

1/4 teaspoon fresh ground black pepper (optional)

DIRECTIONS

1 In a small sauce pan, over a very low flame, add sliced mushrooms and cover.

2 Cook until mushrooms soften, about 8 – 12 minutes. Stir a few times while cooking. You will see the liquid from the mushrooms pooling in the bottom on the pot.

3 Add the can of soup to the mushrooms.

4 Cover and simmer for 3 minutes until mixture is thoroughly heated.

5 Season with pepper.

6 Toast slices of your favorite bread. Pour the mushroom mixture over the bread or serve as a sauce with grilled steak. (Grandma preferred white bread and flank steak or as a topper on a baked potato. Yum!)

TIP

Do not wash mushrooms under water. They tend to absorb water and become mushy.

SHOPPING LIST

Need

☐ Mushrooms

☐ Cream of mushroom soup

May Have on Hand

☐ Pepper

GO FOR "THE GREEN" SAUCE

My friend Donna gave me this recipe while playing golf, hence the name. Serve this sauce with your favorite grilled fish, chicken, or steak. It is also excellent as a dip or topping for a toasted baguette. It is certain to be a "hole in one" recipe.

Servings: 8-10

Prep Time: 15 minutes

Cook Time: None

INGREDIENTS

1/3 cup shallots, coarsely chopped

1/4 cup white wine vinegar

1 cup fresh parsley, chopped

1/2 cup capers, drained

One 2-ounce can flat anchovy fillets, drained or 2 teaspoons of anchovy paste

2 teaspoons fresh thyme, chopped

1 teaspoon salt

1 teaspoon freshly ground black pepper

2/3 cup extra virgin olive oil

SHOPPING LIST

Need

☐ Anchovies (fillets or paste)

☐ Capers

☐ Parsley (fresh)

☐ Shallots

☐ Thyme (fresh)

May Have on Hand

☐ Olive oil (extra virgin)

☐ Vinegar (white wine)

☐ Salt and pepper

DIRECTIONS

1 Chop shallots in a food processor then transfer to a small bowl. Stir in white wine vinegar and set aside

2 Add the remaining ingredients except oil to the food processor and finely chop. Transfer to bowl with shallot and white wine vinegar.

3 Mix with a fork or wire whisk, then whisk in oil.

4 Cover and refrigerate for up to 24 hours before serving.

TIP

Freeze any leftover sauce in ice cube trays. Defrost and serve as needed.

GARLIC BREAD

Garlic bread is a must-have recipe. You might not think about serving garlic bread on a first date; however, garlic is known as an aphrodisiac because it revs up the blood circulation. Wink. Wink.

Aunt Gloria's recipe is one of the best I've ever tasted. Enjoy.

INGREDIENTS

1 loaf French bread, sliced in half

6 cloves garlic, minced

3/4 of a stick unsalted butter

3 tablespoons extra virgin olive oil

DIRECTIONS

1. Preheat oven to 350°F.
2. In a small sauce pan melt butter over low heat. Add garlic and oil. Cook over low heat for 5 minutes. (Be sure to not burn the garlic or the bread will taste bitter.)
3. Let cool, then pour all the ingredients from the pan into a container.
4. Cool in the refrigerator for 20 minutes or until the mixture resembles butter.
5. Slice bread in half and spread the mixture on it.
6. Place bread on a baking sheet and cook in the oven for 5 minutes or until bread is toasted and garlic butter is melted. Watch carefully as it only takes minutes to burn the bread.
7. Serve and enjoy.

Servings: **8**

Prep Time: **25 minutes**

Cook Time: **15 minutes**

SHOPPING LIST

Need

☐ French bread

☐ Garlic

May Have on Hand

☐ Butter

☐ Olive oil (extra virgin)

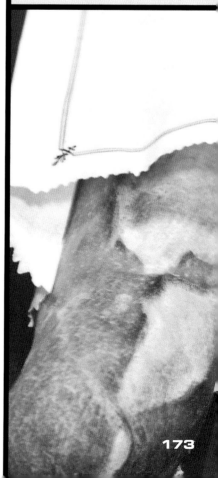

RECYCLED FRIED RICE

No one likes to throw away food. These days everything is so expensive. Why not think of creative ways to reinvent last night's dinner? Try this recipe and you'll be making extra rice just to recycle your leftovers.

INGREDIENTS

1-2 cups cooked rice (rice left over from your Chinese take-out also works great)

1 red pepper, diced

3 scallions, sliced. Reserve 1 tablespoon for garnish.

2 tablespoons vegetable oil

1 crushed chicken bouillon cube

1 cup of hot water

2 slices of cooked bacon, crumbled (optional)

1 tablespoon butter

2 eggs, lightly beaten

2 tablespoon soy sauce

DIRECTIONS

1 In a medium sauté pan, over medium heat, add oil.

2 When oil is hot add your vegetables and sauté, stirring with a wooden spoon for 5 minutes.

3 Add crushed chicken bouillon and water. Mix.

4 Add rice. Add bacon, if desired. Mix.

5 In another non-stick small sauté pan, over medium heat, melt butter then add beaten eggs.

6 Lightly scramble the eggs for 1 minute then add to rice mixture.

7 Top with soy sauce and the reserved scallions.

8 Plate and enjoy.

Servings: **4**

Prep Time: **10 minutes**

Cook Time: **10 minutes**

SHOPPING LIST

Need

☐ Eggs

☐ Red pepper

☐ Rice

☐ Scallions

May Have on Hand

☐ Bullion cube (chicken)

☐ Soy sauce

☐ Vegetable oil

☐ Butter

Optional

☐ Bacon

COUSCOUS ON THE SIDE

Quick and healthy, couscous cooks up in seconds and is a great alternative to a baked potato. It's the perfect accompaniment to my Kitchen Sink Chicken.

INGREDIENTS

1 cup couscous

1 cup chicken stock, broth or water

1 small can garbanzo beans, drained or 1/2 cup

1 small red onion, chopped

1/2 cup black olives

1/2 cup raisins

1/2 cup pine nuts

Juice of 1 lemon

2 tablespoons extra-virgin olive oil

2 tablespoons fresh mint leaves chopped

Salt and black pepper to taste

DIRECTIONS

1 In a pot, bring stock, broth or water to a boil over medium heat. Add couscous then turn off heat. Cover and let sit for 5 minutes.

2 Mix together remaining ingredients then add to cooked couscous. Toss.

3 Fluff up couscous with a fork.

4 Add salt and pepper to taste and enjoy.

Servings: **4**

Prep Time: **15 minutes**

Cook Time: **10 minutes**

SHOPPING LIST

Need

☐ Couscous

☐ Chicken stock

☐ Garbanzo beans

☐ Red onion

☐ Mint leaves

☐ Raisins

☐ Pine nuts

☐ Black olives

May Have on Hand

☐ Lemon

☐ Olive oil

☐ Salt and pepper

KITCHEN SINK CHICKEN Page 113

177

AGLIO E OLIO PASTA (GARLIC AND OLIVE OIL WITH PASTA)

Heat up the night with this Aglio e Olio Pasta recipe. It can hold it's own as a simple T-Man meal.

Servings: 4

Prep Time: 10 minutes

Cook Time: 10 minutes

INGREDIENTS

1 pound package angel hair pasta or linguini, cooked to al dente (see page 245 for how to cook pasta)

6 garlic cloves, minced

1/2 teaspoon red pepper flakes

1/4 cup olive oil

1/4 cup extra virgin olive oil

Salt and black pepper to taste

¼ cup toasted seasoned breadcrumbs

2 tablespoons fresh parsley, chopped (optional)

DIRECTIONS

1 Add a handful of salt to a large pot of boiling water.

2 Add pasta and cook for 2 minutes less than recommended on the package. (I prefer my pasta cooked al dente.)

3 Drain water from pasta. Remember to ladle out one cup of pasta water and set aside.

4 In a large non-stick sauce pan, over very, very low heat, add garlic and pepper flakes and cook for 3 minutes. Mix with a wooden spoon a few times. This cooks and releases the garlic's natural oils. Be careful not to burn.

5 Add oils and cook for 15 additional minutes over medium heat. Toss in cooked pasta and mix, coating pasta in oil.

6 Serve garnished with breadcrumbs and parsley (optional).

SHOPPING LIST

Need
- ☐ Pasta
- ☐ Garlic
- ☐ Breadcrumbs

May Have on Hand
- ☐ Red pepper flakes
- ☐ Olive oil
- ☐ Extra virgin olive oil
- ☐ Salt and pepper

Optional
- ☐ Fresh parsley

HOW TO COOK PASTA Page 245

PESTO PASTA

I was never really much of a pesto fan until I made my own version of this popular sauce with specialty cheeses and good quality extra virgin olive oil.

INGREDIENTS

1 pound rigatoni or other medium pasta shape

2 cups basil leaves, discard stems and pack firmly

3/4 cup Parmesan cheese, grated

3/4 cup Parmigiano-Reggiano cheese, grated

1/2 cup olive oil

1/4 cup extra virgin olive oil 2 tablespoons pine nuts

3 cloves garlic cloves, smashed

2 tablespoon fresh ricotta cheese

DIRECTIONS

1 Cook pasta. (See page 245 for how to prepare pasta.)

2 To make the pesto sauce, add all the ingredients except the ricotta cheese in a food processor or blender. Mix until well blended. Consistency should not be too thick. Add a little additional oil if it is too thick.

3 Spoon the pesto sauce over the warm pasta.

4 Top with fresh ricotta cheese and serve. Enjoy.

Servings: **4**

Prep Time: **10 minutes**

Cook Time: **20 minutes**

SHOPPING LIST

Need

☐ Pasta

☐ Basil

☐ Garlic cloves

☐ Parmigiano-Reggiano cheese

☐ Parmesan cheese

☐ Ricotta cheese

☐ Pine nuts

May Have on Hand

☐ Olive oil

☐ Extra virgin olive oil

PARFAIT
Page 201

CRAZY CAMP COFFEE CAKE Page 185

OMELET
Page 195

PANCAKES

NEW YORK MEETS

CHAPTER 8

BREAKFAST: DAY OR NIGHT?

Breakfast, as they say, is the most important meal of the day and nothing is more important to me than my "You're In a Scramble" recipe. These buttery eggs take seconds to make and when paired with a toasted English muffin, jam and a glass of fresh orange juice they hit the spot, day or night. Any of the recipes in this chapter can easily make an appearance on the lunch or dinner scene. The TASTOSTERONE cook will also find recipes like my pancakes and "Man Quiche" so simple to prepare he may find it hard to get beyond the "Breakfast: Day or Night" chapter.

I also recommend T-Men treat their special someone with an occasional breakfast in bed – morning, noon or night. This gesture of love and appreciation shouldn't be reserved for Mother's Day. It can also put a smile on a sick child's face or cheer up an uncomfortable pregnant wife. I guarantee no one will check the time when the TASTOSTERONE cook brings any one of these amazing dishes bedside.

CRAZY CAMP COFFEE CAKE

Memories are made with food. When my daughter reminisces about her days at Camp Laurel, she tells me about Crazy Camp Coffee Cake. For me, coffee cake brings up memories of my Nana's baking. Since I'm not much of a baker, my version of Nana's recipe is simple, easy and sure to create memories for your little campers.

INGREDIENTS

1 stick of unsalted butter, softened
1 cup sugar
2 eggs
2 cups flour, sifted
1 teaspoon baking powder
1 teaspoon baking soda
1 teaspoon vanilla extract
1 cup sour cream

Nut Mixture
1 teaspoon cinnamon
3/4 cup brown sugar
1/4 cup chopped walnuts
1/4 cup chopped pecans
1/4 cup chocolate chips (optional)

DIRECTIONS

1. Preheat oven to 350°F.
2. Use the pastry blade of a mixer to cream (mix) together butter and sugar on low speed.
3. Add eggs one at a time while mixing.
4. Add flour, baking powder, baking soda, vanilla, and sour cream. Mix until well blended.
5. In a separate bowl, mix together cinnamon, sugar, chopped walnuts/pecans, and chocolate chips (optional).
6. In a loaf or Bundt pan, sprayed with non-stick baking spray, add half the batter, then half the nut mixture. Using a toothpick, swirl the nut mixture into batter. Add the rest of the batter on top of nut mixture, then top with the remainder of the nut mixture.
7. Bake for 40 minutes. To test for doneness slide a toothpick into the cake. When it comes out dry, the cake is done.
8. Let pan cool and remove from pan.
9. Slice and serve.

Servings: **8**

Prep Time: **20 minutes**

Cook Time: **40-50 minutes**

SHOPPING LIST

Need
☐ Sour cream
☐ Pecans
☐ Walnuts

May Have on Hand
☐ Eggs
☐ Butter
☐ Baking powder
☐ Baking soda
☐ Flour
☐ Sugar
☐ Brown sugar
☐ Cinnamon
☐ Vanilla extract

Optional
☐ Chocolate chips

TIPS

You can use a hand mixer if you do not own an electric mixer.

If you plan on baking often, I recommend investing in a Kitchen Aid mixer. It's the sports car of baking and comes in many colors.

BACON, BACON, BACON

I guess if you never made bacon you would think it comes out of the package onto the plate, crispy and lightly browned.

You can pick up a package of precooked bacon, which works great for tossing a few slices on a sandwich or in a salad but T-Men should really know how to make this breakfast staple.

INGREDIENTS

8 slices of bacon (I prefer center cut bacon)

Lots of paper towels

DIRECTIONS

1. Preheat a large sauté pan or grill plate over medium heat.

2. Place bacon slices in pan in a single layer. Cook for 5 - 10 minutes. Turn with tongs a few times, until bacon is to desired crispness.

3. Drain bacon on paper towels.

4. Eat and enjoy.

TIPS

I use a bacon press because it makes the bacon extra crispy.

Use any leftovers in salads and on sandwiches.

Servings: 4

Prep Time: **2 minutes**

Cook Time: **10 minutes**

SHOPPING LIST

Need

☐ Bacon

May Have on Hand

☐ Paper towels

PANCAKES

Who says pancakes need to be perfect? They taste great no matter what they look like, and after topping them with fresh fruit, syrup, and powdered sugar they're gone in seconds.

Here are two tasty versions... one super quick and another for when a T-Man wants to go the extra mile.

MIX IT UP

INGREDIENTS

Pancake mix (It doesn't last forever. Make sure to check the date on the bottom of the box.)
1 teaspoon vanilla extract (That's the love as I call it.)
1 tablespoon unsalted butter

DIRECTIONS

1. Follow the directions on the box of your favorite pancake mix. Add vanilla extract.

2. Heat non-stick fry pan over low heat and add 1 tablespoon unsalted butter. Add additional butter as needed while cooking.

3. With an ice cream scooper or large spoon, scoop out a large spoonful of mix and add it to the pan. Be careful not to crowd the pan. Make sure the pancakes don't touch.

4. When the batter bubbles, flip pancake and cook for another minute.

5. Serve immediately or keep warm on a baking sheet in oven at 200°F until ready to serve.

6. Top with bananas, blueberries, chocolate chips, powdered sugar, and/or syrup.

FROM SCRATCH

INGREDIENTS

2 tablespoons butter
1 cup sifted whole wheat or all-purpose flour
1 teaspoon salt
1 teaspoon baking soda
1 egg
1 cup and 2 tablespoons of low fat buttermilk (If you don't have buttermilk, mix just shy of 1 cup milk with 1 tablespoon lemon juice or white vinegar and let sit for 5 minutes. I prefer buttermilk, but any milk works.)
1 teaspoon vanilla extract

DIRECTIONS

1. Put flour, salt and baking soda in a bowl.

2. Mix in an egg, buttermilk, butter and vanilla. (Don't over mix. A lumpy batter is a good one.)

3. Preheat a griddle or non-stick pan on medium heat for 1 minute.

4. Add 1 tablespoon of butter to pan. With a paper towel spread the butter around the pan, covering the bottom. Be careful not to burn yourself.

5. Pour a little of the batter into the hot pan and form a pancake. Once the batter cake begins to bubble, flip the pancakes over. Cook for an additional 30 seconds per side.

6. Remove from heat and enjoy. For classic pancakes, top with butter and pure Vermont maple syrup.

Servings: **4** Prep Time: **5 minutes** Cook Time: **5 minutes**	**SHOPPING LIST** ☐ Butter ☐ Pancake mix ☐ Vanilla extract

Servings: **4** Prep Time: **15 minutes** Cook Time: **5 minutes**	**SHOPPING LIST** ☐ Egg ☐ Butter ☐ Buttermilk ☐ Flour ☐ Baking soda ☐ Salt ☐ Vanilla extract

FRENCH TOAST

Yesterday's bread is today's dinner. Sometimes the most basic ingredients make the most delicious meals.

Keep it simple sweetie!

INGREDIENTS

1 loaf of day-old bread, sliced (I prefer Challah bread)

2-3 tablespoons unsalted butter

3 eggs, slightly beaten

2 tablespoons milk

1 teaspoon vanilla extract

Toppings (optional)

Cinnamon

Sugar

Preserves or jam

Powdered sugar

Syrup

DIRECTIONS

1 In a large bowl mix eggs, milk and vanilla.

2 Preheat large sauté pan over medium heat and add some of the butter.

3 Dip a slice of bread into egg mixture, then add it to the pan. Cook 2 minutes per side and set aside.

4 Repeat process with additional bread and serve.

Servings: **4**

Prep Time: **10 minutes**

Cook Time: **10 minutes**

SHOPPING LIST

Need

☐ Bread

☐ Eggs

May Have on Hand

☐ Butter

☐ Milk

☐ Vanilla extract

Optional

☐ Syrup

☐ Preserves or jam

☐ Cinnamon

☐ Powdered sugar

☐ Sugar

YOU'RE IN A SCRAMBLE

What's for dinner? You're tired and a little hungry. Reach for the eggs. They're fast and warm. This is a T-Man go-to meal.

The best part about making eggs is that the cleanup takes seconds.

INGREDIENTS

6-8 eggs

3 tablespoons unsalted butter

1/4 cup milk or heavy cream

Dry or fresh herbs (optional)

Cheese, shredded (optional)

Salt and pepper

DIRECTIONS

1 In a large bowl crack open eggs. Add salt, pepper and milk.

2 Heat large skillet over medium heat and add 2 tablespoons butter.

3 Add egg mixture, then cook for 1 minute.

4 Add optional ingredients after one minute and stir with a wooden spoon until eggs are fluffy.

5 Top with 1 tablespoon of butter and mix in.

6 Serve warm with English muffin or toast. (I prefer butter or honey on my bread.)

TIP

While cooking the eggs, the lower the heat you use, the more tender they will be and the lighter they will taste.

Servings: **4**

Prep Time: **5 minutes**

Cook Time: **5 minutes**

SHOPPING LIST

Need

☐ Eggs

☐ Milk or heavy cream

May Have on Hand

☐ Butter

☐ Salt and pepper

Optional

☐ Cheese

☐ Herbs

OMELET

The saying, "To give is to receive" also applies to cooking.

An omelet is the ultimate gift of love. It's a wonderfully simple dish and appreciated around the world as a timeless classic.

Add any ingredients and it takes on an entirely new taste and look.

Servings: 2

Prep Time: **5 minutes**

Cook Time: **5 minutes**

INGREDIENTS

4-6 eggs

1 tablespoon unsalted butter

Salt and pepper

SHOPPING LIST

Need

☐ Eggs

May Have on Hand

☐ Butter

☐ Salt and pepper

DIRECTIONS

1 Heat a large non-stick sauté pan over medium heat. Add 1 tablespoon butter.

2 Crack eggs into a bowl. Add a pinch of salt and pepper and whisk with a fork. Blend until smooth.

3 Pour into pan.

4 Let settle and shake pan. Keep doing this until the liquid is absorbed. At this time, add whatever ingredients you desire or none for a classic omelet.

5 Fold omelet in half or roll into thirds.

6 Flip over to make sure the other side is cooked.

7 Serve warm.

TIP

The sky's the limit so feel free to be creative and experiment with different ingredients from a variety of herbs or vegetables to your favorite meats. Cream cheese is my favorite - it makes for a really creamy omelet.

MAN QUICHE

T-Men men DO cook and eat quiche!

Come on guys, the quiche is a one-pan meal that includes eggs, cheese and other mouthwatering manly ingredients packed into a delicious crust. So, add some cooked steak, ham, chicken, pancetta or sausage and change the stereotype.

INGREDIENTS

1 frozen pie shell
6 eggs, beaten well
8 slices cooked bacon or chopped pancetta, steak, ham, chicken or sausage
1 onion, chopped
1 cup Swiss or Gruyère cheese, shredded
1 1/4 cup milk or cream
1/2 teaspoon salt
1/2 teaspoon pepper
1 tablespoon parsley, chopped

DIRECTIONS

1 Preheat oven to 450°F.

2 Stick a fork in the pie shell several times and with a cooking brush paint it with 1 tablespoon of the egg mixture.

3 Place pie shell on a baking sheet and bake for 5 minutes.

4 Remove from oven and lower temperature to 350°F.

5 Add a tablespoon of oil to a sauté pan and sauté meat with onion. Cook for 5 minutes then transfer to pie shell using a slotted spoon.

6 Pour the egg mixture over the meat.

7 Bake 35 - 40 minutes.

8 Remove from oven and cool.

9 Serve hot or at room temperature.

Servings: **6**

Prep Time: **10 minutes**

Cook Time: **1 hour**

SHOPPING LIST

Need

☐ Cheese (Swiss or Gruyère)
☐ Eggs
☐ Meat
☐ Onion
☐ Parsley
☐ Pie shell

May Have on Hand

☐ Milk or cream
☐ Salt and pepper

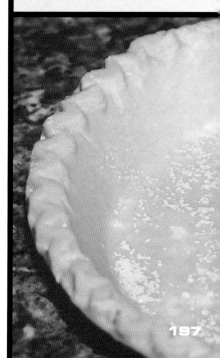

NEW YORK MEETS SCOTLAND

Nothing tastes better than a freshly baked New York City bagel and some sliced smoked salmon. You too can enjoy a piece of the Big Apple no matter where you live.

This recipe is my own twist on the meal, but feel free to make your own combination. Serve with a quality cup of java.

Servings: **2**

Prep Time: **5 minutes**

Cook Time: **None**

INGREDIENTS

2-4 slices Nova lox, cut into thin strips (it's best to buy fresh from the deli counter)

2 fresh bagels

2-3 tablespoons whipped cream cheese

Red onion, thinly sliced

Cucumber, thinly sliced

Tomato, sliced

SHOPPING LIST

Need

- ☐ Nova lox
- ☐ Bagels
- ☐ Cream cheese
- ☐ Cucumber
- ☐ Red onion
- ☐ Tomato

DIRECTIONS

1. Cut bagels in half and lightly toast. Fresh, warm bagels do not require toasting.
2. Smear (NYC term for spread) cream cheese on both sides of your bagels.
3. Top with remaining ingredients.
4. Cut in half and serve.

TIP

Lox refers to salmon which has been cured in a salty brine. Be sure to purchase Nova lox. It has a milder taste because it is lightly smoked and brown sugar is added to the brine.

PARFAIT

Parfaits may sound too wimpy for you to whip up, but please don't deny yourself this yummy treat.

All you need to do is cut up a few pieces of fresh fruit and your parfait is ready to go.

INGREDIENTS

1 cup yogurt, any style, flavored or plain

1 cup fresh fruit, sliced (I prefer bananas, berries and melons)

1/2 cup Kashi Crunch® cereal (or your favorite granola)

DIRECTIONS

1 Add yogurt to a parfait glass, bowl or large wine goblet.

2 Top with fresh fruit.

3 Top fruit with granola.

4 Serve.

TIP

Throw the ingredients into a blender with some protein powder and you have a smoothie.

Servings: **1**

Prep Time: **5 minutes**

Cook Time: **None**

SHOPPING LIST

Need

☐ Cereal

☐ Fruit

☐ Yogurt

DON'T BE SCARED OF SOUFFLÉ

You never know when you might need to cook something for your vegetarian friends. This recipe can be as creative as you desire and is much more filling than serving a bowl of carrots. Your friends will thank you for thinking of them.

INGREDIENTS

1 head of broccoli, chopped
One 15-ounce can cream of mushroom soup
1 cup mayonnaise
2 eggs, slightly beaten
1 medium onion, chopped
1 cup cheddar cheese, shredded
1/4 cup unsalted butter
2 1/2 cups breadcrumbs
Salt

DIRECTIONS

1 Preheat oven to 350°F.

2 Steam broccoli in 1 cup of simmering salted water (1 tablespoon of salt to 3 cups of water) over medium heat. Cover and cook for 5 minutes.

3 Mix together the broccoli, soup, mayonnaise, eggs, onion, and cheese.

4 Grease a casserole dish with butter. Add soufflé mixture, then top with breadcrumbs and slices of butter.

5 Cover and bake for 30 - 40 minutes.

6 Serve warm or at room temperature.

Servings: **6**

Prep Time: **15 minutes**

Cook Time: **40 minutes**

SHOPPING LIST

Need

☐ Eggs

☐ Butter

☐ Cheddar cheese

☐ Broccoli

☐ Onion

☐ Mushroom Soup

☐ Mayonnaise

May Have on Hand

☐ Breadcrumbs

☐ Salt

EAT A PEACH PIE
Page 219

CHOCOLATE BOMB
Page 229

SANDIES
Page 211

**WHIPPED CREAM ON
ANTHING** Page 223

**ICE CREAM
SANDWICHES** Page 227

CHAPTER 9

HAPPY ENDINGS: DESSERT

You're now cooking breakfast day or night, so how about serving dessert first? Remember, there are no rules for the TASTOSTERONE chef. It's such a special treat to start or end a meal with something sweet. There are so many reasons to conquer the recipes in this chapter! In life, you will find a dessert can get you through the worst of days and help you to celebrate the best of them.

No matter when you enjoy these delightful treats, you will appreciate how easy they are to make and how delicious they taste. I do not consider myself a baker because most of my desserts require little or no baking. For example, my "Apple Crisp Ice Cream Topping" is just a few sugary sweet ingredients heated slightly. My "Over the Top Ice Cream Sandwiches" are made and enjoyed by guests in minutes. These recipes are as much fun to make as they are to eat.

BUTTER COOKIES SQUARES

My Aunt Helen and Uncle Milton have been married for over 60 years. I'm sure my great grandmother's cookies must have something to do with their successful marriage. They are buttery delicious!

INGREDIENTS

2 sticks unsalted butter

1 cup brown sugar

2 cups all-purpose flour

1 teaspoon baking powder

1 egg yolk and 1 egg white, separated (see Tip)

1 teaspoon cinnamon

1 teaspoon vanilla extract

1 1/2 cups walnuts, coarsely chopped

DIRECTIONS

1. Preheat oven to 350°F. Spray baking sheet (11 inch x 15 inch) with nonstick spray.

2. Mix all ingredients except egg whites and walnuts.

3. Press mixture onto a baking sheet. It should be about 1 inch deep and cover the entire baking sheet. If you wish you can use a smaller pan for thicker cookies.

4. Beat egg white. With a basting brush, brush the whisked egg white on top of batter then top with walnuts. Slightly press the nuts into the batter.

5. Bake for 20 minutes.

6. Remove from oven and cut into 2 inch squares. Let cool in pan for 15 minutes before removing.

7. Remove from pan, plate and enjoy.

TIP

How to separate eggs:
Hand method - Crack the egg into your hand, letting the whites pass through your fingers into a small bowl while keeping the yolk intact in your hand. Place the yolk into a separate small bowl.
Hide and Seek method - Crack egg open over a small bowl, only allowing the whites to escape into a small bowl. Place yolk into a separate small bowl.
Fishing method - Crack egg into a small bowl being careful not to break the yolk. With a slotted spoon, fish out the yolk and place it in another small bowl.

SLICED BUTTER COOKIES

Quick and easy, slice and bake cookies are available at your supermarket. Although that shortcut is fine in a pinch, my recipe may take more time but will create more memories. Keep in mind that this is a great opportunity to teach those young T-Men that baking can be fun.

INGREDIENTS

3 eggs
1/2 cup orange juice
2 sticks unsalted butter
2 teaspoons baking powder
3/4 cup sugar
4 1/4 cups flour

DIRECTIONS

1. Preheat oven to 400°F.
2. In a large bowl, combine the baking powder, sugar and flour. With an electric mixer, using a pastry blade (if possible), cut in the butter. Mix for about two minutes until batter looks like little peas, not totally blended. (See Tip.)
3. Add juice and eggs until all ingredients are combined, about 1 minute on medium speed. Don't over mix.
4. Roll out the dough to make a long log (2 inches in diameter) and bake on greased bake sheet for 10 minutes.
5. Remove from the oven and cut into 2 inch slices while hot. Let cool.
6. Serve and enjoy.

TIP

Often a recipe will call for you to "cut in" shortening or butter. "Cutting in" means incorporating shortening or butter into the flour in such a way that little lumps of the raw fat remain whole within the flour mixture, hence the "pea size" balls of dough.

The easiest way to accomplish this is to use a large fork and press the butter into dry ingredients or use an electric mixer fitted with a pastry attachment.

Servings: **6**

Prep Time: **10 minutes**

Cook Time: **10 minutes**

SHOPPING LIST

Need

☐ Butter

☐ Eggs

☐ Orange juice

May Have on Hand

☐ Baking powder

☐ Flour

☐ Sugar

SANDIES

Sandies are a cookie classic. Serve with your favorite coffee, cappuccino or espresso.

INGREDIENTS

4 1/2 cups all purpose-flour

1 pound unsalted butter, softened
(leave out for about 30 minutes to soften before baking)

1 teaspoon salt

2 teaspoons vanilla extract

1 cup walnuts, roughly chopped

1 cup powdered sugar, plus 2 tablespoons for garnish

DIRECTIONS

1. Preheat oven to 350°F.
2. Cream sugar and butter, then add the remaining ingredients.
3. Shape batter into 1 inch balls and place 2 inches apart on a nonstick baking pan. (I place a sheet of parchment paper on the pan to make cleanup a snap.)
4. Bake for 20 minutes.
5. Remove from oven and sprinkle with powdered sugar.
6. Let cool, then serve.

Servings: **8**

Prep Time: **15 minutes**

Cook Time: **20 minutes**

SHOPPING LIST

Need

☐ Butter

☐ Powdered sugar

☐ Walnuts

May Have on Hand

☐ Flour

☐ Salt

☐ Vanilla extract

TIP

The way to cream your ingredients is to use your mixer at medium speed and beat the ingredients together until they are light and fluffy.

This technique helps the sugar to dissolve and beats air into the butter giving it a fluffy texture.

BROWNIES

No woman can resist chocolate, and as any T-Man knows, you can never have enough brownie points!

INGREDIENTS

18 graham cracker cookies, crushed (about 2 cups) (see Tip)

One 8-ounce can sweetened condensed milk

1/2 - 3/4 cup chocolate bits or chocolate chips

1 teaspoon vanilla extract

1/2 cup walnuts, chopped

DIRECTIONS

1. Preheat oven to 350°F.
2. In a large bowl, mix all ingredients. Consistency should be wet, thick and sticky.
3. Spray a 9 inch square pan with nonstick bake spray. Pour mixture into pan.
4. Bake for 30 minutes.
5. Remove from the oven, let cool for 10 minutes, and then cut into 2 inch squares and plate and enjoy.

TIP

To crush graham cracker cookies, place them in a plastic bag and close. Make sure no air is left in bag.

Using a heavy spoon, rolling pin or even a hammer (a T-Man's favorite tool) crush the cookies in the bag until they are broken crumbs.

Servings: **6**

Prep Time: **10 minutes**

Cook Time: **30 minutes**

SHOPPING LIST

Need

☐ Graham cracker cookies

☐ Condensed milk

☐ Chocolate bits

☐ Walnuts (chopped)

May Have on Hand

☐ Vanilla extract

CHOCOLATE BITES

Children love spending time in the kitchen with mom or dad and nothing beats the moment they make a dish their own.

My girlfriend's son bakes these bites often and they go as fast as he can make them!

INGREDIENTS

20 wonton wrappers, rolled into a cigar shape

5 tablespoons chocolate hazelnut spread
(I prefer the one and only Nutella)

1/2 cup vegetable oil

3 tablespoons powdered sugar

DIRECTIONS

1 Take a wonton wrapper and place 1/2 teaspoon of chocolate hazelnut spread on top.

2 Roll the wonton into a long tubular shape. (You may need to wet your fingers with some water to achieve this.) Continue the process until all the wontons are filled.

3 In a medium-sized pot, heat oil over high heat. Using a slotted spoon, carefully place wontons into oil and cook until they are golden brown (1-2 minutes). Don't crowd the pot. With tongs or a slotted spoon, remove from oil and set onto paper towels to absorb excess oil.

4 Sprinkle with powdered sugar and serve warm or at room temperature.

TIPS

There are a great selection of splatter screens available that you can place on top of pots and pans when cooking to avoid oil splattering or being burned.

If you have an old spice jar, clean it out and fill it with confectioner's sugar. It's great to have on hand when you bake as well as when you make pancakes or French toast.

Servings: **4**

Prep Time: **5 minutes**

Cook Time: **10 minutes**

SHOPPING LIST

Need

☐ Chocolate hazelnut spread

☐ Wonton wrappers

May Have on Hand

☐ Powdered sugar

☐ Vegetable oil

CHOCOLATE RING CAKE

This dessert really satisfies those chocolate cravings. Surely our T-Man will make someone's night special with this decadent dessert.

Servings: **6**

Prep Time: **10 minutes**

Cook Time: **45 minutes**

INGREDIENTS

1/4 pound unsalted butter

1/2 cup sugar

1 cup all-purpose flour

4 eggs

1 cup chocolate syrup (I prefer the Hershey's brand that comes in a can, but it is sometimes difficult to find)

1 teaspoon vanilla extract

2 tablespoons powdered sugar

DIRECTIONS

1 Preheat oven 350°F.

2 Melt butter in a small sauce pan over low heat.

3 In a large bowl, add melted butter. With an electric mixer, beat in sugar and flour until blended, about 2 minutes. In same bowl, add eggs, chocolate and vanilla. Beat for an additional 2 minutes until blended.

4 Spray ring/Bundt pan with bake spray. Pour mixture into the pan.

5 Bake 45 minutes or until a toothpick comes out clean.

6 Remove from pan and cool.

7 Sprinkle with powdered sugar.

SHOPPING LIST

Need

☐ Chocolate syrup

☐ Eggs

May Have on Hand

☐ Butter

☐ Flour

☐ Powdered sugar

☐ Sugar

☐ Vanilla extract

"EAT A PEACH" PIE

I was always afraid to bake pies until an original T-Man showed me just how easy baking one can be with his peach pie. I'm finding out that many men enjoy baking.

Could they really have the sweetest tooth of all?

INGREDIENTS

1 frozen pie shell
1/4 stick unsalted butter, softened (leave out at room temperature)
1/3 cup sugar
1/3 cup all-purpose flour
3 tablespoons water
3- 4 ripe peaches, peeled, pitted and thinly sliced
1 pint of ice cream (I prefer Häagen-Dazs Five Ingredients vanilla ice cream or any quality brand that doesn't contain preservatives)

Topping
3 tablespoons cinnamon
2 tablespoons sugar

DIRECTIONS

1. Preheat oven to 425°F.
2. Using a fork, poke holes all over the bottom and sides of the pie shell, about 20 marks. Place in oven and bake for 5 minutes.
3. Remove pie shell from oven and turn temperature down to 375°F.
4. Using an electric mixer with a pastry attachment, mix together butter, sugar, flour, and water until batter resembles large peas or marbles. Do not overmix.
5. Place peach slices into the pie shell. Evenly disperse the peaches covering the bottom of the shell.
6. Top with flour mixture.
7. Line a baking sheet with foil to save on cleanup time.
8. Place the pie on the baking sheet and bake for 60 minutes.
9. Combine cinnamon and sugar in a separate bowl.
10. Remove the pie from the oven and top with the cinnamon and sugar while hot.
11. Serve warm with vanilla ice cream. Enjoy.

Servings: **8**

Prep Time: **10 minutes**

Cook Time: **1 hour**

SHOPPING LIST

Need
- ☐ Pie shell (frozen)
- ☐ Peaches
- ☐ Ice cream

May Have on Hand
- ☐ Butter
- ☐ Cinnamon
- ☐ Flour
- ☐ Sugar

TIP

You can replace peaches with eight ripe plums or apples for a twist on the recipe.

CHOCOLATE WAFER ICEBOX CAKE

I have been making this cake for years. This cake brings family together and creates many new memories.

This is the ultimate T-Man recipe, perfect for any occasion. By the way, don't tell anyone how simple it is... there's no baking required!

You will also find the recipe for this cake on the side of the Nabisco box. I included it because I believe this one needs to be reintroduced for this generation to enjoy. It is a perfect beginner's recipe. Why mess with an original?

INGREDIENTS

2 packages chocolate wafer cookies (I prefer Nabisco Famous Chocolate Wafers)

2 cups whipped cream (see recipe on page 223)

1 cup chopped walnuts

DIRECTIONS

1 Make whipped cream.

2 Arrange cookies on a 12 inch round cake plate. You will be alternating cookies with whipped cream, as if you were making the first level of a log house. The cake is complete when all the cookies are used.

3 Cover the entire cake with the whipped cream (make sure you completely cover all chocolate wafers). Cover with plastic wrap and refrigerate for a minimum of 4 hours.

4 Remove from the refrigerator and sprinkle with nuts. Cut cake on an angle to expose the layers when serving.

5 Enjoy.

Servings: **8**

Prep Time: **20 minutes**
(Refrigerate for 4 hours to overnight.)

Cook Time: **None**

SHOPPING LIST

Need

☐ Chocolate wafers

☐ Chopped walnuts

☐ Whipped cream

WHIPPED CREAM
Page 223

WHIPPED CREAM ON ANYTHING

Fresh whipped cream makes anything taste amazing.
It can be whipped up in seconds, flattering any dessert.

INGREDIENTS

1 pint heavy cream

1 tablespoon sugar

1 teaspoon vanilla extract

DIRECTIONS

1. Place a medium-size bowl and mixer attachments in freezer for at least 10 minutes for flawless whipped cream. I promise you it will work every time. (I prefer a copper bowl. See Tip.)

2. Remove bowl and mixer attachments from freezer and pour cream, sugar and vanilla into the bowl.

3. Using an electric mixer, beat on medium-high speed for 5 minutes until cream forms ribbons and peaks.

4. Don't overmix or you will have butter for tomorrow's breakfast toast.

5. Enjoy.

TIP

The bowl you use makes a difference when you are whipping cream. Copper bowls produce creamy foam that is harder to overbeat than the foam produced using glass or stainless steel bowls.

Servings: **6**

Prep Time: **15 minutes**

Cook Time: **None**

SHOPPING LIST

Need

☐ Heavy cream

May Have on Hand

☐ Sugar

☐ Vanilla extract

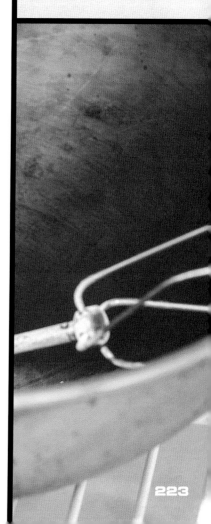

APPLE CRISP ICE CREAM TOPPING

Not many people have the time to bake in the kitchen, however we all love homemade desserts. This apple crisp topping paired with some vanilla bean ice cream takes no time at all to prepare.

I prefer to use Granny Smith apples in the topping, but any fruit will do. Choose what's in season and you won't go wrong.

INGREDIENTS

1/2 cup flour
1 cup rolled oats (do not use instant oatmeal)
1/2 cup light brown sugar
1/2 cup brown sugar
3 tablespoons cinnamon
1/4 teaspoon salt
1 stick butter cut into 1 inch slices
5 Granny Smith apples, peeled, cored and cut into 6 wedges
Juice of 1 small lemon
2 tablespoons sugar
1 pint of ice cream (I prefer vanilla)

DIRECTIONS

1 Preheat oven to 350°F.

2 Mix all ingredients together except ice cream.

3 Spread a 2 inch thick layer of the mixture into the bottom of a 9 inch x 13 inch baking dish greased with butter.

4 Bake for 45 minutes until apples are soft.

5 Remove from oven. Add a scoopful of crisp topping then ice cream, alternating layers of each, to a parfait or large glass (even a pilsner glass works in a pinch.)

6 Serve warm. Enjoy.

Servings: **8**

Prep Time: **10 minutes**

Cook Time: **45 minutes**

SHOPPING LIST

Need

☐ Apples

☐ Oats

☐ Light brown sugar

☐ Brown sugar

☐ Ice cream

May Have on Hand

☐ Butter

☐ Sugar

☐ Cinnamon

☐ Flour

☐ Lemon

☐ Salt

TIP

Apple crisp can be made ahead of time and stored in the refrigerator so you can have it on hand for those late night trips to the fridge or freezer.

OVER THE TOP
ICE CREAM SANDWICHES

Ice cream sandwiches make the perfect snack whether they're devoured while watching the Monday Night Football game or at your child's birthday party. They are so yummy in your tummy. I once made this statement to my daughter's fifth grade class and, needless to say, she never let me live it down.

INGREDIENTS

1 package cookies (I look for a homemade style like Tate cookies, but feel free to use any flavor. I like chocolate chip.)

1 pint frozen yogurt or ice cream, lightly softened

Any toppings (I prefer crushed waffles cones, sprinkles, chocolate chips, mini M&M's, chopped Snickers bars, crushed Oreo cookies, and chopped nuts.)

DIRECTIONS

1. Spread softened (not melted) ice cream in between two cookies to make a sandwich.
2. Place your preferred toppings on individual plates. Roll sides of the sandwiches in toppings.
3. Tightly wrap cookie in plastic wrap then foil and freeze for 1 hour. (See Tip)
4. Unwrap and enjoy.

TIP

Be careful that the ice cream/yogurt doesn't get too soft or it will develop freezer burn. Freezer burn spoils the taste of any food.

These ice cream sandwiches can last up to a month in the freezer if wrapped properly, but they never last in my house because they taste too good.

Servings: **4**

Prep Time: **10 minutes** (Refrigeration time 1 hour)

Cook Time: **None**

SHOPPING LIST

Need

☐ Cookies

☐ Ice cream or frozen yogurt

☐ Toppings

CHOCOLATE BOMB

My friends Samantha and Jon have been married for a few years. Jon is the cook and Samantha the cleaner. Together, they cook up successful dinner parties. This dessert is Jon's special treat for guests. Now you can enjoy it, too.

INGREDIENTS

6 ounces bittersweet chocolate
1/2 stick (4 tablespoons) unsalted butter
1 cup sugar
2 large eggs
1 1/2 cups heavy cream
1 cup whipping cream
1 teaspoon vanilla extract
Pinch of salt
1/4 cup all-purpose flour
Unsweetened cocoa powder for garnish

DIRECTIONS

1. Preheat oven to 350°F.

2. Melt the chocolate and butter in the top of a double boiler *(See Tips.)* When melted set aside to cool.

3. Using an electric mixer with a paddle attachment or by hand using a spoon in a large bowl, mix the sugar and eggs until color lightens, about 1 minute.

4. Pour the cooled chocolate/butter mixture beat into the mixer or bowl then stir in the heavy cream, vanilla and salt. Beat well, scraping the ingredients from the sides of the bowl as you mix.

5. Add the flour and mix until blended.

6. Divide the mixture between four 6-ounce ovenproof cappuccino cups or any style cup or small bowl. Fill to 1/4 inch below the rim of the cup.

7. Place cups on a baking sheet and bake for 30 minutes or just until the tops of the cake begin to crack. Do not over bake. The tops should be crisp and the interior soft.

8. Remove from oven and let cool for 15 minutes. While cooling, make the whipped cream. Whip the cream until it forms soft peaks, about 5 minutes. Don't over whip or it will turn into butter. You could also use whipped cream from a can to save time.

9. Place a dollop of the flavored whipped cream onto each warm cup and garnish with a dusting of cocoa powder.

10. Serve warm and enjoy.

Servings: 4

Prep Time: 15 minutes

Cook Time: 30 minutes

SHOPPING LIST

Need
- ☐ Chocolate (bittersweet)
- ☐ Cocoa powder
- ☐ Eggs
- ☐ Heavy cream
- ☐ Whipping cream

May Have on Hand
- ☐ Butter
- ☐ Flour
- ☐ Sugar
- ☐ Salt
- ☐ Vanilla

TIP

A double boiler consists of a bowl placed on top of a pan of simmering water. The bowl does not touch the water, but creates a seal with the bottom pan to trap the steam produced by the simmering water. The trapped steam keeps the top bowl warm. Inside the top bowl, you can melt chocolate without worrying that it will stick and burn.

You can buy a double boiler, but it's easy to make one at home. All you need is a mixing bowl (preferably glass/Pyrex or metal) and a saucepan. The pan and bowl should fit tightly together; you don't want a gap between the bowl and the saucepan, nor do you want a bowl that sits precariously. To use the double boiler, add water to the pan and bring it to a simmer, then place the bowl on top and fill it with whatever you intend to cook or melt.

APPLE TARTE PIZZA

I love this dessert, which I first enjoyed at Auberge du Dully in Switzerland. It was difficult to find some of the ingredients in the U.S. so here is my version.

INGREDIENTS

1 cup plus 5 tablespoons flour, divided
1 stick of unsalted butter (cold)
Pinch of salt
1 cup water
1 tablespoon sugar
3 tablespoons apple or pear butter
6 tablespoons heavy cream

DIRECTIONS

1. Preheat oven to 425°F.
2. To make the tarte dough, in a large bowl add 1 cup flour, salt, butter, and water. Using an electric mixer, fitted with a paddle attachment, mix on medium speed until the butter appears to crumble into pea-sized morsels (about 3 minutes).
3. Remove the dough mixture from the bowl and roll into a large ball. Set on a plate, cover with plastic wrap and place in the refrigerator for 30 minutes.
4. Spray a spring form pan (8 inch - 11 inch diameter) with non-stick bake spray.
5. Sprinkle 2 tablespoons of flour onto a surface and rolling pin.
6. Take dough from refrigerator and set it onto the floured surface and roll out with the rolling pin. (Dough should be rolled out very thin, like a thin crusted pizza pie.)
7. Carefully lift dough and transfer onto the greased pan.
8. Sprinkle the top of the dough evenly with the remaining 3 tablespoons of flour and sugar.
9. Using a basting brush or the back of a soup spoon, spread a paper thin layer of apple or pear butter on dough.
10. Pour heavy cream on top.
11. Bake in the oven for 10 minutes or until golden brown.
12. Serve warm and enjoy.

Servings: **8**

Prep Time: **15 minutes**

Cook Time: **10 minutes**

SHOPPING LIST

Need

☐ Apple or pear butter
☐ Heavy cream

May Have on Hand

☐ Butter
☐ Flour
☐ Salt
☐ Sugar

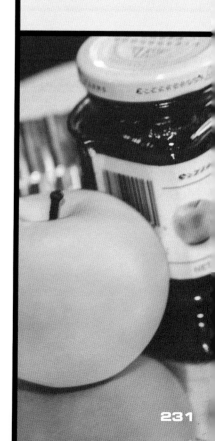

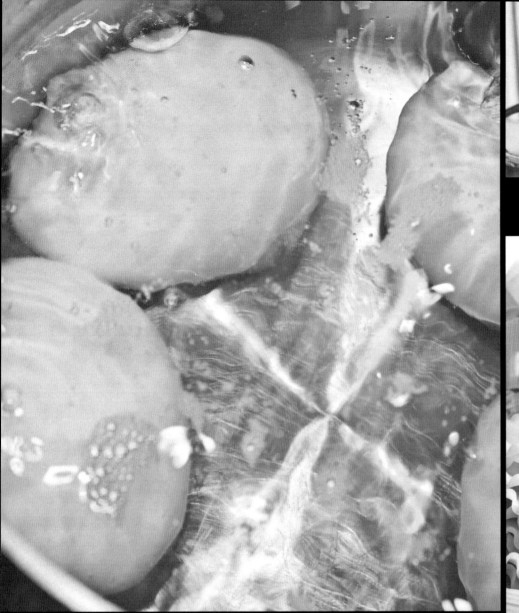

BOILED EGGS
Page 235

BAKED POTATOES
Page 237

SWEET POTATOES OR YAMS

PASTA
Page 245

TOMATO SAUCE

CHAPTER 10
REALLY? HOW TO BOIL AN EGG? REALLY?

In this chapter, I share how to's for the newbie cook. Learn how to avoid being embarrassed by the sideline chef asking, "Really? You don't know how to boil an egg. Really?"

There really are no rights or wrongs to cooking in this book, but I hope these recipes and tips lay the groundwork for years of confident cooking.

BOILED EGGS

There are so many ways to eat boiled eggs. You can slice them and add to a salad, mash them with mayonnaise, salt and pepper for an egg salad sandwich or just eat them plain with a little salt.

The list is endless once you are able to boil an egg – your road to TASTOSTERONE is paved.

Servings: **3**

Prep Time: **2 minutes**

Cook Time: **12 minutes**

INGREDIENTS

6 fresh eggs

Salt and black pepper to taste

DIRECTIONS

1. Fill a medium pot halfway with cold water.

2. Gently place the eggs in the pot, careful not to break.

3. Turn burner to medium heat, bring the water to a boil. Bubbles will form when water boils.

4. Turn the heat down slightly and simmer for 6 minutes. After 6 minutes, turn off the heat and cover the pot with a lid. Let sit for 6 additional minutes.

5. Pour out water and replace with cold tap water, leaving the eggs in the water bath. Allow eggs to cool (about 5 minutes).

6. Peel eggs and discard shells.

7. Serve topped with salt and pepper. Enjoy.

SHOPPING LIST

Need

☐ Eggs

May Have on Hand

☐ Salt and pepper

BAKED POTATOES

Baked potatoes are a steakhouse favorite and a healthy, delicious side dish. This T-Man favorite can be mastered in no time.

INGREDIENTS

2 large Idaho potatoes

Toppings
(Any kind or amount will do. These are my favorites.)

Crispy bacon (see page 187 for recipe)

Sour cream

Pat of butter

Parmesan cheese, freshly grated

Chives or scallions, chopped

Hot sauce

Salt and pepper

DIRECTIONS

1 Preheat oven to 375°F.

2 Scrub skin of potato with a rough sided sponge and remove any blemishes or dirt. Pat dry.

3 Using a knife, cut the potato down the center, but not all the way through.

4 Place potatoes directly on rack in oven for 45 - 60 minutes. The longer you cook the crunchier the skin gets.

5 Split open and serve hot. Top with butter, salt, pepper, and/ or any of your favorite toppings.

Servings: **2**

Prep Time: **2 minutes**

Cook Time: **60 minutes**

SHOPPING LIST

Need
☐ Potatoes

Optional
☐ Bacon
☐ Sour cream
☐ Butter
☐ Parmesan cheese
☐ Chives
☐ Hot sauce
☐ Salt and pepper

SWEET POTATOES OR YAMS

What's the difference between a sweet potato and a yam? Who knows?

These little treats are filled with antioxidants and your little T's will only taste the sweetness.

Servings: **2**

Prep Time: **2 minutes**

Cook Time:
45 minutes - 1 hour

INGREDIENTS

2 large sweet potatoes or yams

Toppings
(I prefer these because they go well with the sweetness of the potatoes or yams)

Pat of butter

Cinnamon/sugar

Candied ginger

Mini marshmallows

Salt and black pepper

SHOPPING LIST

Need

☐ Sweet potatoes or yams

Optional

☐ Butter

☐ Cinnamon/sugar

☐ Candied ginger

☐ Mini marshmallows

☐ Salt and pepper

DIRECTIONS

1 Preheat toaster oven or conventional oven to 375°F.

2 Scrub skin of potato with a rough sided sponge and remove any blemishes or dirt. Pat dry.

3 Using a knife, cut the potato down the center, but not all the way through.

4 Place potatoes directly on rack in oven for 45 - 60 minutes. The longer you cook the crunchier the skin gets.

5 Add toppings. If adding marshmallows, after topping place the potatoes or yams back in oven until marshmallows are melted (about 1 minute).

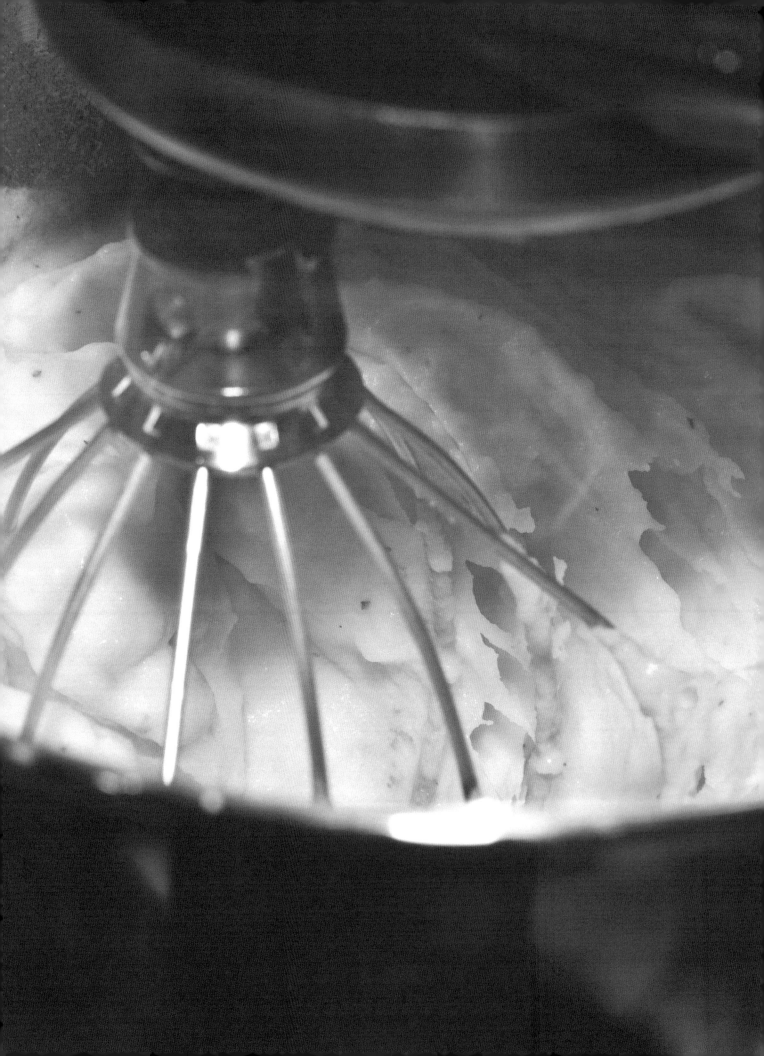

MASHED POTATOES

Gone are the days of perfect mashed potatoes. Don't strive for perfection, T-Men, TASTOSTERONE lowers the bar and raises the taste.

Servings: **6**

Prep Time: **10 minutes**

Cook Time: **30 minutes**

INGREDIENTS

2 pounds baby yellow or fingerling potatoes

1 cup milk

1/4 cup heavy cream

3/4 stick (6 tablespoons) unsalted butter, softened

1/2 - 1 tablespoon of salt to taste

2 teaspoons black pepper

Handful of kosher salt

SHOPPING LIST

Need

☐ Potatoes

☐ Milk

☐ Heavy cream

☐ Butter

May Have on Hand

☐ Salt and pepper

DIRECTIONS

1　Cut potatoes in halves.

2　Fill a large pot with cold water. Add a handful of kosher salt and potatoes. Turn burner on high and bring to a boil.

3　Once the water boils, turn down heat to low and simmer the potatoes for about 10 minutes until tender when pierced with a fork (not too soft.)

4　Drain the water from the pot and place the potatoes in a large bowl.

5　Add softened butter, milk and cream. Using an electric mixer or food processor with a metal attachment, mash the potatoes until they reach a creamy consistency. Sprinkle with salt and pepper.

TIPS

If making ahead of time, cover the warm potatoes with plastic wrap then cover with foil.

If reheating your mashed potatoes, you may need to add additional milk or butter to get that creamy consistency again.

RICE

There are many types of rice (long grain, brown, basmati, and sushi.) Each one of them has specific cooking instructions. All of them, however, will either instruct you to rinse the rice first or soak it in cold water.

Simply read and follow the instructions on the packaging and you'll do great.

INGREDIENTS

2 cups water

1 cup rice

1/2 teaspoon kosher salt (optional)

Salt and pepper to taste

DIRECTIONS

1. In a medium pot, bring water to a boil over high heat.
2. Add rice and salt and stir. Reduce heat to a low simmer and cover.
3. Cook for 20 minutes. Don't peek. If you do, the steam will release and the rice will lose some of it's moisture.
4. After 20 minutes, use a wooden spoon to push rice to one side of the pot to see if there is any liquid left under the rice. If all water is absorbed, turn off the heat and let rest covered for 5 minutes.
5. If water is still visible in the pot, cover and cook a few more minutes until it has evaporated then turn off the heat and let rest covered for 5 minutes.
6. Fluff with a fork and season with salt and pepper to taste. Enjoy.

Servings: **4**

Prep Time: **5 minutes**

Cook Time: **20 minutes**

SHOPPING LIST

Need

☐ Rice

May Have on Hand

☐ Salt and pepper

☐ Paper towels

TIP

Never stir rice while it's cooking or it will become gummy.

PASTA

Pasta comes in all shapes and sizes and that's why the cooking times vary.

It is important to read the package to determine how long the pasta needs to boil in order to ensure it's cooked al dente and not overcooked into a ball of mush.

INGREDIENTS

Pasta

Handful of kosher salt

DIRECTIONS

1. In a large pot filled halfway with water (roughly 8 quarts), add a handful of kosher salt. Bring to a boil.

2. Add pasta and stir. Set a timer for the recommended cooking time on the package. Carve 2 minutes off that time for perfect al dente pasta.

3. Once the pasta and water boil again, turn the heat down to a low boil. Stir occasionally in order to prevent pasta from sticking together.

4. When timer rings, before draining the pasta, take a mug or measuring cup and scoop out a cup of the pasta water. Set aside.

5. Place a strainer in your sink. Using kitchen mitts or a few hand towels remove the pot from the stove and pour water and pasta into the strainer.

6. Now you are ready to toss the pasta with your favorite sauce (i.e. tomato, flavored olive oil or butter).

Servings: **4**

Prep Time: **5 minutes**

Cook Time:
Varies with each type of pasta, anywhere from 2 - 18 minutes

SHOPPING LIST

Need

☐ Pasta

May Have on Hand

☐ Salt

TIP

If pasta sticks together, toss with some of the reserved pasta water, adding a little at a time.

Adding reserved pasta water will help your sauce adhere to the noodles.

TOMATO SAUCE

Gravy or sauce? Call it what you may, on any given Sunday there's nothing better than the smell of homemade sauce filling the house. This one takes no time to make.

Servings: **2**

Prep Time: **2 minutes**

Cook Time: **10 minutes**

INGREDIENTS

2 tablespoons olive oil

1 garlic clove

One 28-ounce can crushed tomatoes

One 15-ounce can chopped tomatoes

1 small can tomato paste

1/2 cup Marsala wine

Pinch of red pepper flakes

1/2 cup water

1 bay leaf

DIRECTIONS

1. Heat the oil in a large pot over medium heat. When the oil is hot, sauté the garlic for 1 minute, then remove. This will flavor the oil. Be careful not to burn the garlic or the oil will become bitter.

2. Add the rest of the ingredients to the pot and stir. Bring to a boil, then lower heat and simmer covered for 30 minutes. Stir the sauce a few times while it cooks.

3. Remove the bay leaf and season to taste.

4. Enjoy over pasta or other TASTOSTERONE recipes that call for tomato sauce.

SHOPPING LIST

Need

☐ Crushed tomatoes

☐ Chopped tomatoes

☐ Tomato paste

May Have on Hand

☐ Olive oil

☐ Garlic

☐ Marsala wine

☐ Red pepper

☐ Bay leaf

TOOLS
Page 260

HOW TO REMOVE AN AVOCADO PIT Page 253

WHAT DOES MIX BY HAND MEAN?

TERMS

CHAPTER 11

COOKING TIPS, TERMS, TOOLS, AND TECHNIQUES

As I've said throughout this book, there really are no rules for the TASTOSTERONE cook.

I do, however, recommend that you follow some simple guidelines that will make your cooking journey easier. Take them or leave them – you'll cook up delicious meals even if you refuse a little guidance along the way.

In this chapter, I also include my "Dirty Dozen" common cooking mistakes. You may think they're silly and you would never make them in a million years, but trust me I've been there and am happy to share my blunders and mistakes so that as a TASTOSTERONE cook you can navigate the kitchen with confidence and ease.

WHEN COOKING, DO...

- Relax. You can do this!
- Check with your guests for any special dietary needs when planning your menu.
- Read the instructions before starting.
- Take stock and measure your ingredients before you start.
- Prepare as much as you can before you begin cooking.
- Make sure you have enough space in the refrigerator for leftovers.
- Taste as you go.
- Have fun!

WHEN COOKING, DON'T...

- Take yourself too seriously.
- Fear experimenting.
- Use too many pots, dishes or bowls.
- Let the grumpy guest ruin your good time.

... AND NEVER EVER LEAVE A MESSY KITCHEN!

THE DIRTY DOZEN:
HOW TO AVOID COMMON COOKING MISTAKES

1 TASTE AS YOU GO

Too much or too little salt can ruin a dish. When you add salt or any spice for that matter, wait until it blends with the other ingredients, then taste again (about 2-3 minutes).

2 TURN IT ON

Preheating an oven saves time. Use an oven thermometer to make sure the oven is at the recommended temperature before you cook or bake. An oven thermometer can stay in the oven all the time.

3 KNOW THE RULES

Prep, prep, prep saves time and mistakes. Make sure you have all the ingredients on hand and reserve what might be needed later in the recipe. Remember marinating meat or fish can take minutes or days.

4 SHARPEN YOUR TOOLS

Sharp tools save trips to the emergency room. Believe it, you will get fewer cuts (hopefully none) with sharper knives since the knife does the work for you. There is no need to push down hard on the knife, which may cause the food and knife to slip away.

5 HEAT IT UP

Make sure your pan/oil is hot enough to begin cooking. Place the handle of a wooden spoon in the oil and if bubbles form around the handle then your oil is ready.

6 KEEP IT JUICY

Let your meat rest for 15 minutes before serving or slicing. The time off will make the meat tender and juicy. If you cut the meat right as it comes right out of the oven, the juices will release, making the meat dry and chewy.

7 GO AGAINST THE GRAIN

Slice meat against the direction of the muscle fiber. By doing this, meat will be tender. Look at the direction of how the grain is going and slice in the opposite direction.

8 BE READY

Don't start baking or cooking and see that the recipe calls for the butter to be softened or left out at room temperature. The microwave can be a great time saver in a pinch.

9 MIX IT UP

Don't overmix your ingredients when cooking or baking, as they will break down and result in tough cookies and mushy muffins.

10 USE A LIGHT HAND

If you like salt you can always add more, but you'll never be able to end the complaining coming from a disgruntled guest who prefers a low-sodium diet.

11 BE PATIENT

When searing any kind of meat it will naturally release from the pan when it's ready. If you try to turn it over too soon, you lose will all the flavor and it won't look pretty. And who needs an ugly piece of meat?

12 RELEASE AND RELOAD

If the flavor of your dish is off, it's better to start with a clean slate than to be unhappy with your end result. We've all been there.

SHORTCUTS

"FLOUR" POWER

Store seasoned flour (2 cups flour, 3 tablespoons salt and 1 teaspoon black pepper) in a plastic storage bag. This saves getting these ingredients out each time you need them and saves a lot of mess in the kitchen. Label the bag and store in freezer. No expiration date.

Store flour sifter in plastic bag so you don't have to wash it after each use and flour dust won't get all over your cupboard.

BUTTER ME UP

Melted butter will keep a while if left out of refrigerator. Use a pastry brush to "paint" butter on toast, bagels, skillet, baking pan or whatever. A 1-inch new paintbrush will do just fine, and is less expensive then baking brushes.

THROW IN THE TOWEL

When you need to drain out a little bit of oil from a pot, instead of pouring the hot oil into the sink or garbage, hold a few paper towels in a pair of tongs, wipe out most of the oil, run under cold water and discard.

COUNT ON ME

Instead of measuring out liquid tablespoon ingredients, count to three when pouring out the liquid – it should equal a tablespoon.

MASH IT

Rest the side of a chef's knife on a garlic clove and using your palm, mash it. This will get out frustration and also mashes the garlic beautifully.

TOP IT!

To caramelize onions and other vegetables as toppings for your steak, burger or onion soup, cook them in oil, covered, over very, very low heat. Stir and watch the magic!

GREEN AND MEAN

When choosing an avocado, it should be soft. Pop out the core (the little piece at the top of the avocado) if it's green, it's fresh; if it's brown, the avocado will be brown as well. Produce guys, don't hate me! If you purchase avocados and they are too hard, place them on the counter for a few days to soften. Never refrigerate an avocado. (See page 11 for my Great Guacamole recipe.)

NUTS!

Don't neglect your nuts. When toasting nuts watch them or they can burn, making your dish taste very bitter.

MORE NUTS!

If you have nuts leftover from a recipe, store the excess in the freezer. You can even chop them before freezing to save on preparation time.

HOW TO REMOVE AN AVOCADO PIT

1. Cut the avocado in half lengthwise around the pit and separate halves.

2. Strike the pit with a sharp knife, using enough force for it to wedge halfway into the pit.

3. With the edge of the knife, twist the pit out and either save it to place in guacamole to slow down the browning process, or throw it away.

4. Scoop out the avocado from its shell.

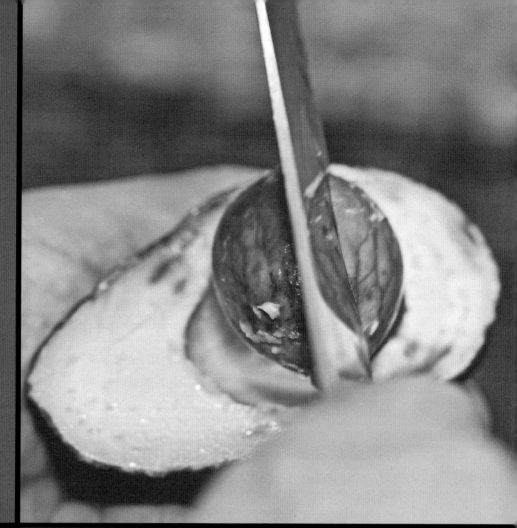

WHAT DOES "MIX BY HAND" MEAN?

When I say mix by hand, like meatloaf mixture mix, I mean with your hands.

When cake or cookie mix directions say "mix by hand" it means to use a fork, spoon or even a hand held mixer set on low speed to mix the ingredients.

One day my daughter wanted to bake cookies, she made cookies and followed the direction "mix by hand." So, that's what she did, and boy were her hands sticky, but the cookies came out delicious.

See, it all works out in the end.

Always remember, cooking should be fun and never taken too seriously.

HOW TO CLEAN A CHICKEN

Not my favorite thing to do, but it's important to do it correctly.

1. Unwrap chicken and place in the sink.

2. Discard the neck and gizzards. (The gizzards are usually found in the inside cavity of the chicken.) If your butcher is cutting up the chicken for you, you can ask for him to also discard the neck and gizzards.

3. Line a large tray with paper towels.

4. Rinse the chicken thoroughly under cold water. You can also use a tablespoon of kosher salt to help clean the chicken. Make sure to wash off the salt during this step.

5. Place the chicken onto the paper towels and dry. Blot the top with more towels.

6. Place cleaned chicken on a clean plate. Throw away the used paper towels and wash the sink and tray with antibacterial soap.

7. Prepare your favorite TASTOSTERONE chicken dinner recipe.

HOW TO GREASE A PAN

There are many ways to grease a pan depending on your taste and whether you're baking or cooking. Greasing a pan helps cut down on clean up time by ensuring food doesn't burn or stick to the pan. Remember that depending on the size of the pan you may need more or less flour or butter. Use your judgment, but don't overdo it as you don't want to change the taste of your food.

OPTION 1

1 - 2 tablespoons unsalted butter
Paper towel
2 tablespoons flour (for baking desserts)

Take softened butter and use the paper towel to spread butter all over the sides and bottom of pan to thinly coat the entire surface. If baking sweets, I recommend sprinkling flour on top of the butter. Shake pan so the flour coats a thin layer on top of butter and excess comes off.

OPTION 2

Non-stick spray oil
Baking spray with flour

Spray your pan with non-stick cooking spray and for baking use one with flour added.
(I prefer PAM Cooking Spray. They make a variety from non-stick to baking.)

HOW TO SET A TABLE

1. Set down the placemat.

2. Place the dinner plate in the center of the placemat.

3. Both forks are placed on the left side of the plate. The smaller fork furthest from the plate is for salad. The larger fork next to the plate is for the dinner.

4. The dinner knife is placed on the right side. The blade should face the plate.

5. Place the spoon to the right of the dinner knife.

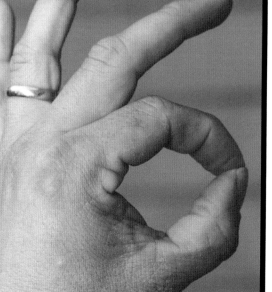

TESTING... 1, 2, 3... TESTING...

MEAT THERMOMETER

A meat thermometer can be used for all foods, not just meat. It's a helpful tool to measure the internal temperature of your cooked meat and poultry to ensure that any harmful bacteria is destroyed.

THE FINGER TEST

Many chefs check the doneness of meat by the way it feels when touched with their fingers. Once you get used to using this easy method, you'll have mouthwatering meat cooked just the way you and your guests prefer in no time. In addition to this simple finger test, you can also test by using a meat thermometer or cutting into the meat with a knife. The only downfall is that you'll lose some of those tasty juices if you cut into the meat.

With the guide below, you can use the way your own flesh feels to test for the doneness of meat.

WELL DONE
Gently press the tip of your pinky and your thumb together. Again feel the fleshy area below the thumb. It should feel quite firm.

MEDIUM
Press the tip of your ring finger and your thumb together. The flesh beneath the thumb should give a little more.

MEDIUM RARE
Gently press the tip of your middle finger to the tip of your thumb.

RARE
Press the tip of your index finger to the tip of your thumb. The fleshy area below the thumb should give a bit.

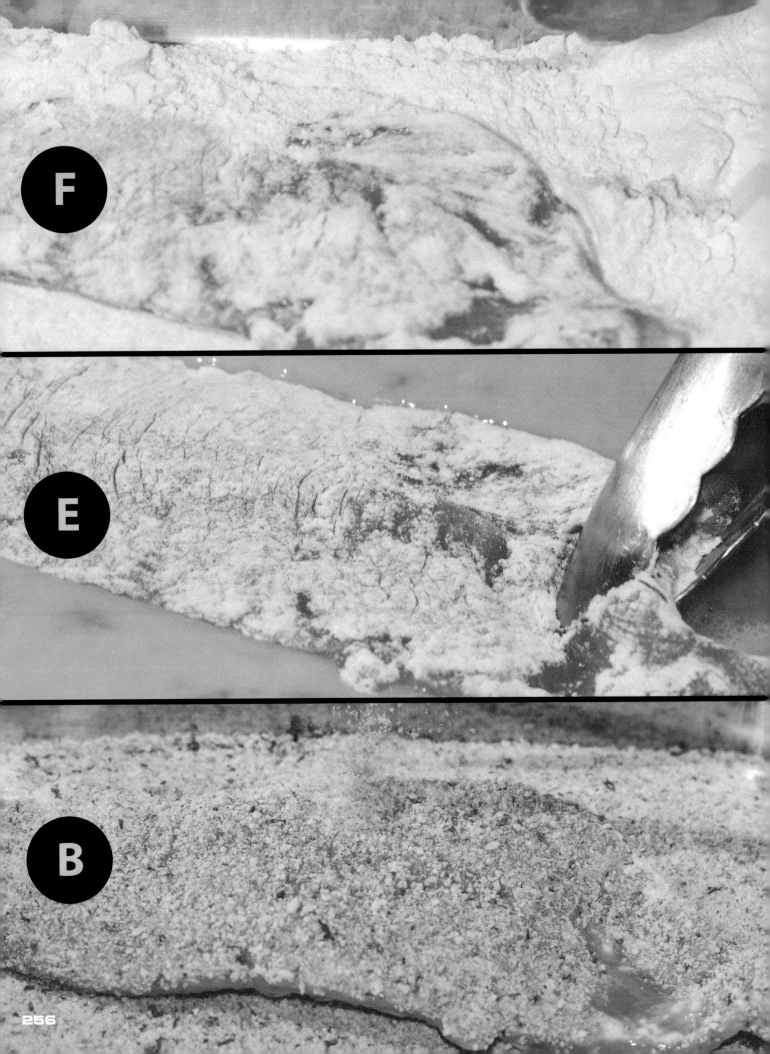

Remember F.E.B. and you'll never be in doubt when preparing TASTOSTERONE dinners. When baking or frying up some of my favorite recipes like Chicken Bites on page 25 or Chicken Parmesan on page 51, I came up with F.E.B. This acronym stands for the ingredients flour, egg and breadcrumbs.

To make the F.E.B. combination, prepare your flour, egg yolk and breadcrumbs in three separate bowls. First you dip and coat your chicken, fish, meat or vegetables in flour, then in egg, and then in breadcrumbs. Once coated in the ingredients, your recipe will then call for frying or baking the meal. Some recipes may suggest that you pound your meat before coating.

You can also change up the flavor of your F.E.B. meals by adding or experimenting with ingredients. Try using a variety of breadcrumbs from Italian seasoned to Panko Japanese-style ones. If like a spicy twist to your food, add a pinch of cayenne pepper, or if you prefer a punch of flavor, add some finely chopped fresh herbs like oregano and basil.

Come up with your own acronyms when prepping and cooking meals, and you'll find you cut down on time and trouble.

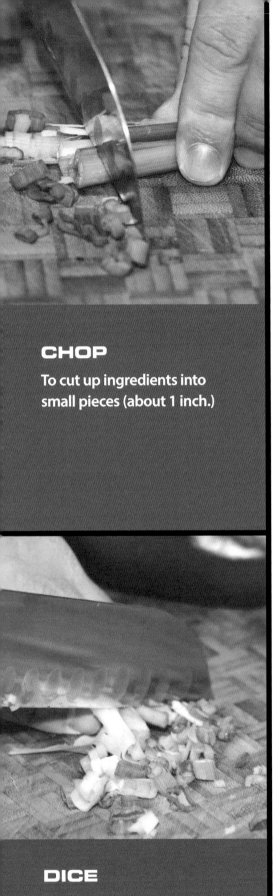

CHOP

To cut up ingredients into small pieces (about 1 inch.)

DICE

To cut up ingredients into very small pieces.

TERMS

AL DENTE
To cook pasta or rice till slightly hard. The best way of accomplishing pasta al dente is to cut 2 minutes off the cooking directions.

BASTE
To add flavor to any food by moistening it during cooking. Just spoon any liquid left in the bottom of the pan and pour it on top of whatever is cooking. Basting keeps meat moist and adds flavor. I baste meat or fish about every 15 minutes, especially if the meat needs to cook low and slow for hours.

BEAT
To add air to an ingredient by using a mixer, whisk or use my favorite tool - a simple fork. Place fork in ingredients (i.e. an egg or cream) and stir with your wrist in a quick, circular motion.

BLEND
To combine ingredients well, but make sure not to overmix them so they become unrecognizable.

BOIL
To cook a liquid on high heat over stove burner, until it bubbles.

BROIL
To set the oven to the broil setting and cook food on the top rack or bottom broiler of the oven. When broiling, food needs to be watched very carefully to prevent a fire or burning.

COAT
To cover your food in an ingredient. This process usually involves flour, breadcrumbs and eggs. Dip food into these ingredients separately and then shake off the excess.

CHOP
To cut up ingredients into small pieces (about 1 inch).

CREAM
To mix until smooth.

CUBE
To cut ingredients into 1-3 inch pieces, depending on the recipe. Most of the time cutting into cubes refers to handling meat.

DEGLAZE
To dissolve the burnt dried-out cooking pieces of seared meats or vegetables and juices left on the base and sides of a pan, add a little water, stock or wine to the pan. (I prefer wine. The alcohol in wine causes the bits to release very easily.) Over high heat, use

a wooden spoon to scrape off the dried bits and dissolve most of the added liquid. Not only does this technique add lots of flavor to any dish, but when it comes time for clean up rarely do you need to scrub a pan for more than a few minutes. Deglazing is one of my favorite techniques in the kitchen.

DICE

To cut up ingredients into very small pieces.

FRY

To pour oil in a pre-heated frying pan, over high heat, and cook ingredients. Add food when hot. It's always a good idea to have paper towels set aside on a plate to place the fried food when it's done cooking in the oil. Make sure to add any seasoning (i.e. salt, pepper, squeeze of lemon, etc.) when your food is still hot for best absorption.

GRIND

To place ingredients in a food processor to make smaller pieces.

MARINATE

To rest food before cooking in a liquid made with a combination of several ingredients that add flavor. This step can range from a few minutes to a few days. It is important not to marinate some foods too long (refer to recipe times) because the marinade can act as a cooking agent.

MINCE

To cut up ingredients into very, very, very small pieces.

MIX BY HAND

To use a fork, spoon, mixer or your hands to combine all the ingredients.

SEAR

To place food on a very hot preheated pan for a short period of time to add a crust to the outside of the food without cooking entirely through.

SIMMER

Simmering is a food preparation technique in which foods are cooked in hot liquids kept at or just below the boiling point of water. To keep a pot simmering, bring your food to a boil and then reduce the heat to a point where the formation of bubbles has all but ceased.

SLICE

To cut food into long narrow pieces. Length and width can vary. Slicing into very, very thin strips is called "to julienne".

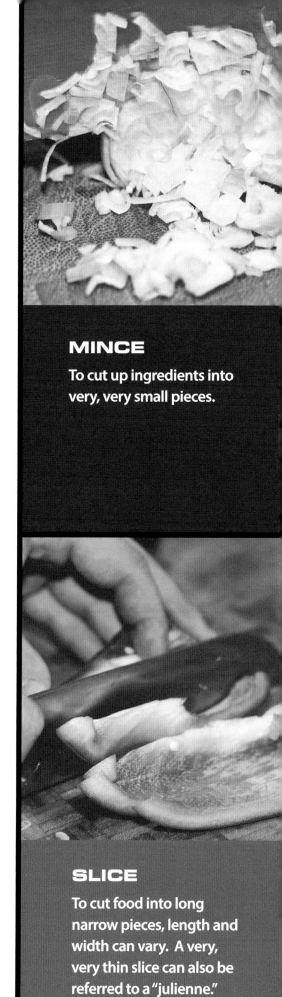

MINCE

To cut up ingredients into very, very small pieces.

SLICE

To cut food into long narrow pieces, length and width can vary. A very, very thin slice can also be referred to a "julienne."

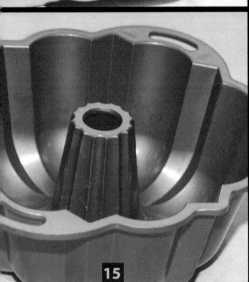

TOOLS

No matter what level of cook you consider yourself to be, you'll need some basic equipment to prepare a meal. Owning the right tools gets the job done.

Your budget may dictate the brands you purchase, but with so many great resources available online and if you do your "homework," you'll find quality cooking equipment at deeply discounted prices. Shop around.

MUST-HAVES
- Toaster/toaster oven
- Tea kettle
- Microwave
- Timer

POTS AND PANS
- Small and large non-stick frying pans (1)
- Small, medium and large sauce pans with covers (2)
- Medium and large soup or stew pot with covers (3)
- Double boiler with cover
- Non-stick baking sheet

- Tart pan
- Non-stick bundt pan (15)
- Non-stick cake pan
- Cupcake non-stick pan
- Aluminum or disposable pans in a variety of shapes and sizes (16)
- Ovenproof baking dishes

UTENSILS
- Bread knife (11)
- Paring knife (14)
- Chef's knife (13)
- Set of steak knives
- Kitchen shears

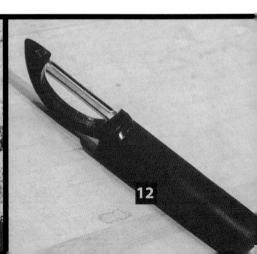

- Small and large tongs
- Slotted spoon
- Large and small wooden spoons
- Spatula
- Measuring spoons and cups
- Whisk

THE BIG GUNS
- Mixer, hand or electric (4)
- Food processor (5)
- Commercial coffee maker
- Panini maker (6)
- Fondue pot and/or set (7)
- Electric carving knife
- Emulsion mixer
- Crock pot (8)
- Juicer
- George Foreman grill

MISCELLANEOUS
- Stackable mixing bowls
- Peeler (12)
- Grater (10)

- Colander
- Steamer (9)
- Meat thermometer
- Oven thermometer
- Small and large sealable storage and freezer bags
- Aluminum foil
- Parchment paper
- Plastic wrap
- Wooden skewers
- Cutting boards

For most of the items above, I recommend the following brands: KitchenAid (mixer), Cuisinart (food processor), Breville (toaster/ blender/panini maker), Le Creuset (fondue pot), All-Clad (cookware), and Le Creuset pots and casserole pans, CorningWare (glass and ceramics), Wusthof, Henckels or even Cutco for great value (knives).

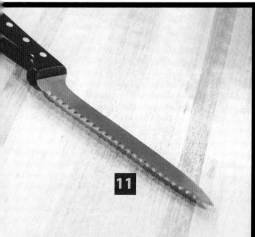

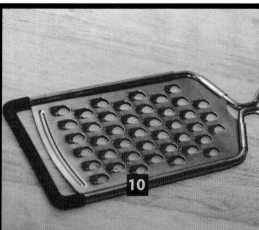

CHAPTER 12

TAKE STOCK: FOODS AND SPICES YOU NEED

Stocking your kitchen with ingredients can be a daunting task when you start from scratch. My shopping list may look intimidating but is important to save the TASTOSTERONE cook time and money in the long run. You may not need all the items listed from the get-go, so review what your recipes call for and maybe consider just buying some staple supplies and ingredients. Down the road, building up your arsenal of ingredients will be key to making sure you're cooking with ease and confidence any time, day or night.

This chapter includes my suggestions for stocking your spice rack, cabinets, pantry, fridge, and freezer. Many of the items listed in this chapter have expiration dates that you should check so food doesn't spoil. To preserve them longer, some items like breads, cereals and nuts can be frozen and defrosted right before using. Also, make sure to store pantry items in airtight containers or bags in a cool place to preserve freshness.

BAKING

Baking soda
Baking powder
Cornstarch
Vegetable shortening
All-purpose flour
Sugar
Powdered/confectioner's sugar
Brown sugar
Light brown sugar
Cocoa powder (unsweetened)
Baking chocolate (unsweetened)
Chocolate chips

SPICE RACK

Kosher salt
Sea salt
Table salt
Ground black pepper
Peppercorns
Vanilla extract
Ground cinnamon
Basil
Oregano
Chili powder
Dry mustard
Paprika
Thyme
Tarragon
Dill
Bay leaves
Garlic powder
Bouillon cubes (chicken and vegetable)

CUPBOARD

Bread
Breadcrumbs (seasoned and unseasoned)
Rice
Quinoa
Couscous
Pasta
Tomato paste
Tomato sauce
Canned tomatoes
Peanut butter
Jelly
Nutella
Canned tuna
Raisins
Cereal
Oats
Cookies: chocolate chip, graham crackers, chocolate wafers
Chocolate syrup
Chicken and beef stock
Canned soups
Canned beans
Canned or jarred olives
Dried fruit: cranberries, prunes, apricots
Lime juice
Honey
Maple syrup
Tea
Coffee
Dried onion soup mix
Pancake mix (check expiration date)

OIL & VINEGARS

Vegetable oil
Canola oil
Olive oil
Extra virgin olive oil
Red wine vinegar
White wine vinegar
Balsamic vinegar
Non-stick cooking spray
Non-stick bake spray
White and red wine for cooking

REFRIGERATOR

(Be sure to check the shelf life of food.)
Milk
Juice
Eggs
Butter
Cheeses
Yogurt
Cream cheese
Sour cream
Nuts (keep in fridge or freezer)
Deli meats
Prosciutto
Salami
Bacon
Fruit: lemon, limes, berries, melon, peaches, prunes
Vegetables: mushrooms, peppers, lettuce, carrots, celery, onions

CONDIMENTS

(Once opened, these must be refrigerated.)

Mayonnaise

Ketchup

Mustard (Dijon, spicy and brown)

Soy sauce

Heinz chili sauce

Hot sauce

Teriyaki sauce

Anchovy paste

Worcestershire sauce

Barbecue sauce

Salsa

Sweet and sour sauce

Plum sauce

FREEZER

(Just because they're frozen doesn't mean they last forever.)

Frozen vegetables: French cut green beans, creamed spinach, chopped spinach, peas, corn, pearl onions, corn/corn on the cob

Gyoza or dumplings

Ground beef/chicken/lamb/veal (any ground beef of choice)

Chicken breasts

Shrimp

Pizza

Ice cream/frozen yogurt

Piecrust

PRODUCE

Fruit: oranges, apples, avocados, bananas, tomatoes (Yes! Tomatoes and avocados are fruit.)

Vegetables: onions, potatoes, sweet potatoes or yams, and garlic

TIPS

Onions and garlic don't get along and need to be stored separately.

All vegetables and fruit are best stored in a cool dry place. Fruit stores well on top of a counter.

Never, never, never refrigerate tomatoes! It's just wrong.

To quickly ripen fruit, place it in a paper bag on the counter. After a day or so, your fruit will ripen.

BREAKFAST LUNCH DINNER

CHAPTER 13
MENU SUGGESTIONS

A menu should reflect a cook's taste, but also make his guests feel comfortable by including a few of their favorite foods. You may also want to consider adding a few vegetable dishes to your menu if any of your guests are vegetarians or vegans. When inviting guests over, it's always best to ask your guests if they have any special dietary needs (i.e. vegetarian, vegan, gluten-free, restrictions due to allergies or religion). A T-Man shouldn't fall flat in the kitchen because he overlooked his guests' menu preferences. Be sure to include a variety of foods on your menu that will accommodate everyone.

GAME TIME

TOO FULL FOR DINNER

WARM IT UP

GET TOGETHER

COMFORT FOOD

APPLAUSE

Celebrities are just like us; they push shopping carts down aisles; they make reservations at their favorite restaurants; and they enjoy sitting down to a delicious meal. At the end of the day, whether they're enjoying a meal made in their very own kitchen or dining in a top rated restaurant, most celebs know nothing beats a home cooked meal.

I included this T-Man Quiz in the cookbook to test your knowledge on which celebrities are finding the time and confidence to cook things up in the kitchen. If you know a celebrity T-Man, tweet us @Tastosterone. We want to hear about those star-studded T-Men.

CHAPTER 14

THE T-MAN QUIZ: GUESS WHAT CELEBRITY MEN COOK?

This is a list of celebrity men who cook and don't cook. Who has TASTOSTERONE?

Go ahead quiz yourself and friends! I bet you'll be surprised by the results on the back of this page. No peeking!

Y N		Y N		Y N	
☐ ☐	Sebastian Cabot	☐ ☐	Moby	☐ ☐	Johnny Depp
☐ ☐	Daniel Craig	☐ ☐	Clint Eastwood	☐ ☐	Daniel Craig
☐ ☐	Danny Kaye	☐ ☐	Bill Cosby	☐ ☐	Matthew Modine
☐ ☐	Josh Brolin	☐ ☐	Justin Bieber	☐ ☐	Tim Gunn
☐ ☐	Stedman Graham	☐ ☐	Alex Rodriquez	☐ ☐	Harrison Ford
☐ ☐	Tobey Maguire	☐ ☐	Derek Jeter	☐ ☐	Tom Cruise
☐ ☐	Vincent Price	☐ ☐	David Wright	☐ ☐	Elton John
☐ ☐	Sylvester Stallone	☐ ☐	Josh Groban	☐ ☐	Jack Black
☐ ☐	Christopher Walken	☐ ☐	Jamie Redknapp	☐ ☐	David Beckham
☐ ☐	James Spader	☐ ☐	Brad Pitt	☐ ☐	Keanu Reeves
☐ ☐	The Situation	☐ ☐	Jackie Chan	☐ ☐	Prince William
☐ ☐	Jionni LaValle	☐ ☐	Chris Brown	☐ ☐	Pierce Brosnan
☐ ☐	Jeff Brazier	☐ ☐	Corey Feldman	☐ ☐	Drake
☐ ☐	Chris Martin	☐ ☐	President Bill Clinton	☐ ☐	Jon Bon Jovi
☐ ☐	Sir Paul McCartney	☐ ☐	Coolio	☐ ☐	Bradley Cooper
☐ ☐	Ben Affleck	☐ ☐	Hugh Hefner	☐ ☐	Mario Lopez
☐ ☐	Richard Gere	☐ ☐	Jake Gyllenhaal	☐ ☐	Will Ferrell
☐ ☐	William Shatner	☐ ☐	Matthew McConaughey	☐ ☐	Jay-Z
☐ ☐	Robert Pattinson	☐ ☐	Eminem	☐ ☐	Adam Levine
☐ ☐	Tom Hanks	☐ ☐	John Travolta	☐ ☐	Michael Bublé

THE T-MAN QUIZ:
GUESS WHAT CELEBRITY MEN COOK?

ANSWERS

Y	N	
■	☐	Sebastian Cabot
■	☐	Daniel Craig
☐	■	Danny Kaye
■	☐	Josh Brolin
☐	■	Stedman Graham
■	☐	Tobey Maguire
■	☐	Vincent Price
☐	■	Sylvester Stallone
■	☐	Christopher Walken
■	☐	James Spader
■	☐	The Situation
■	☐	Jionni LaValle
■	☐	Jeff Brazier
☐	■	Chris Martin
■	☐	Sir Paul McCartney
■	☐	Ben Affleck
☐	■	Richard Gere
■	☐	William Shatner
☐	■	Robert Pattinson
■	☐	Tom Hanks

Y	N	
■	☐	Moby
■	☐	Clint Eastwood
■	☐	Bill Cosby
☐	■	Justin Bieber
■	☐	Alex Rodriquez
■	☐	Derek Jeter
■	☐	David Wright
■	☐	Josh Groban
■	☐	Jamie Redknapp
☐	■	Brad Pitt
■	☐	Jackie Chan
■	☐	Chris Brown
■	☐	Corey Feldman
■	☐	President Bill Clinton
■	☐	Coolio
☐	■	Hugh Hefner
■	☐	Jake Gyllenhaal
■	☐	Matthew McConaughey
■	☐	Eminem
■	☐	John Travolta

Y	N	
■	☐	Johnny Depp
■	☐	Daniel Craig
■	☐	Matthew Modine
■	☐	Tim Gunn
■	☐	Harrison Ford
■	☐	Tom Cruise
☐	■	Elton John
■	☐	Jack Black
■	☐	David Beckham
■	☐	Keanu Reeves
■	☐	Prince William
■	☐	Pierce Brosnan
■	☐	Drake
☐	■	Jon Bon Jovi
■	☐	Bradley Cooper
■	☐	Mario Lopez
■	☐	Will Ferrell
■	☐	Jay-Z
■	☐	Adam Levine
■	☐	Michael Bublé

ABOUT THE AUTHOR

Debra Levy Picard started cooking at the age of 14 to help her busy working parents get dinner on the table. As a child, she was intrigued with cooking and remembers fondly watching Julia Child and writing down her recipes and preparing them for her family. Debra is a self-taught chef who has spent years traveling and adapting recipes from around the world.

Influenced by her family, living abroad, career, a love of the game of golf, and her passion for cooking and entertaining, Debra wrote TASTOSTERONE: The Best Cookbook for Men to provide a man with a road map of supplies, tips, and recipes for navigating around the kitchen.

Debra has seen cooking come a long way with the development of revolutionary kitchen gadgets, nationally syndicated food shows and the internet, but she knows that one ingredient is still missing– men. Although there are many professional male chefs, the role of cook at home still falls on the woman. After doing some market research, Debra found that men have a desire to enter the kitchen, but the motivation, support and resources are just not available.

Recent statistics also show that women 30 and under are now taking on other roles around the home and ditching the cooking. This means that men must dive into the role of cook or prepare to lead a bland life. As Debra sees it, "If you can't stand the heat, get out of the kitchen," and it's only going to get hotter once men gain the confidence to cook.

INDEX

ACKNOWLEDGEMENTS

TASTOSTERONE: THE BEST COOKBOOK FOR MEN would not have been possible without the support of my beautiful parents, Barbara and Stan Levy. Thanks to them, I have many memories of conversations around the kitchen table, traveling and dining at fine restaurants. They have inspired my love of food and cooking.

I also want to thank my friends, Jennifer Smiga of inBLOOM Communications, Maryann Small of Muse Designworks and photographer Stephan Lowy. This mighty team helped me to stay focused on the prize; believing in me, the cookbook and TASTOSTERONE the brand. They encouraged me to remain committed, patient and open-minded, not willing to quit and to push forward. My gratitude to them always for helping me to follow my dream.

Thank you as well to my editors at The Write Room, LLC.

I am also forever grateful to the men who discover TASTOSTERONE. Enjoy entertaining and nurturing your children, family and friends with your new talent and skill. Let's hear it for the boys!

Made in the USA
Charleston, SC
10 April 2013